THE HERB GARDEN GOURMET

GROW HERBS, EAT WELL, AND BE GREEN

TIM HAAS JAN BEANE

SOURCEBOOKS, INC.®
NAPERVILLE, ILLINOIS

Published by Sourcebooks, Inc.
P.O. Box 4410, Naperville, Illinois 60567-4410
(630) 961-3900
Fax: (630) 961-2168

Originally published as *From Basil to Thyme* in 2005 by Champion Press, Ltd.

ISBN-13: 978-1-60751-909-6

Printed and bound in the United States of America.

DEDICATION

Jan's Dedication

I would like to dedicate my portion of this book to my beloved grandparents. I had the good fortune to live next door to them so their influence on me has been and still is very profound. They were born in 1912 and 1914 into a world that was very different from the one we live in today. They, along with most people at that time, lived off the land. Wastefulness was simply unheard of. Reusing, recycling, and repairing happened every day. Isn't that what the "green" revolution is all about?

My grandfather grew most of the food we ate. My grandmother was always canning, freezing, and pickling the results of his labor. There was a barn with pasture land and cows. This translated into milk and later beef in the freezer. My grandfather always heated his house with wood he harvested off the land, never cutting down a live tree. I fondly recall how each fall he would plant a patch of alfalfa for the rabbits. He knew that with winter coming, their food would be harder to come by. Once I sought his advice about planting some cherry trees. He smiled and told me to be sure to plant enough for my family and the birds. He knew how carefully the birds monitor cherries as they are about to ripen. Now that I think about it, he never had a cherry tree on his property! Every fall he would purchase a farmer's almanac and study it through the winter. When spring came, he always planted by the signs, and he always had a successful garden. He lived to the ripe age of 92, never once suffering from a stroke, heart attack, or cancer. In fact he enjoyed good health until he was stricken with Alzheimer's disease. There is nothing sadder to see someone you love decline to the point of not being able to take care of himself. My brothers fondly called him "the great one." I wonder how many people today think of their loved ones that way.

My grandmother was simply the best. She was a hard worker in whatever she was doing. She made all her clothes and most of mine. With much fondness I remember how she would lay the fabric across the kitchen table and pin the pattern to it. When she would cut around the pattern, she would push the scrap fabric off the table out of her way. Well, I loved to play with those scraps. I have always loved color so I had bags of scrap fabric sorted according to color. Later these pieces of fabric became quilts and coats of many colors. At her memorial service, I think the dress she had on was the only dress I had ever seen her in that she didn't make. Her cooking was outstanding. She loved to bake pies and cakes, often experimenting to give us new flavors. I know that if only she were here today, she would have been a part of this book. In fact, she would have been a part of all my endeavors—that's how close we were.

If you are a grandparent, please pass on knowledge you have acquired to your grandchildren, and if you have grandparents, please make them a part of your life always. I miss those two people, and as long as I live they will live in my memory.

Tim's Dedication

I lovingly dedicate my portion of this book to a great lady from my past. Her name was Betty Feezor and she lived in the Charlotte, North Carolina, area. I never had the good fortune to meet her, yet she was invited into my home five times a week. Betty Feezor was probably one of the first people to have a how-to program on television. She cooked, sewed, and performed various needle crafts for a thirty-minute show. Why do you think she left such an impression on me?

My young life was rather turbulent. My earliest memories of being at home with my mother are filled with the things that little boys do: play and imagine. My mother would get her daily chores finished so she could watch Betty's show each weekday. She would tell me when it was time for the show each day, and if she forgot I would become upset to think I had missed it. I loved to listen to Betty give instructions on different cooking techniques. I loved to hear the sound of the spoon or whatever implement she was using as it would hit the side of the bowl or pot. I would try to imitate those sounds by getting into my mother's kitchen cabinets and dragging out her cookware. Sometime later my parents chose to separate and my life took on a frenzy of unhappiness. Whenever and wherever I was at the time, I would try to watch Betty Feezor. She brought stability to my life, which otherwise was lacking stability. I know she never knew about me, but I always felt a bond with her.

I often wonder if the people in our lives have any idea how much they are loved. Do we tell them or just leave it to chance? Well Betty, I have always loved you. I thank you from the bottom of my heart for the comfort you brought me and for pioneering the way for the rest of us who yearn to share with others tips and techniques on lifestyle.

From Our Table to Yours

CONTENTS

ACKNOWLEDGMENTS

We wish to take this opportunity to acknowledge some very special people in our lives. First of all, thank you to everyone at Sourcebooks for all your hard work in making this the most incredible cooking and gardening book available. We feel privileged to be associated with such an outstanding publishing company.

Thanks go out to Jimmy and Donna Dean, Lorianne Crook, and Nathalie Dupree for their kind words and support. It is so nice to have such good friends in the business to call on when needed. We will always remember these acts of kindness. CJ, thank you for motivating us to continue to pursue our dreams, which has culminated in this book and other endeavors as well. And thanks to Donna Haas (Tim's dear wife) for not giving up on us when things seemed bleak. Hopefully we have it this time.

A special thanks to Greg Springs and Barry Gribbon at Homerun Entertainment for believing in us. Our show *From the Garden to the Kitchen with Tim and Jan* has been made possible because of your confidence and expertise. We look forward to a long and prosperous relationship with you. We could not think of a finer production company to be in association with.

To our friends at the RFD network, a heartfelt thank you. What a great network to have our show on! We especially thank you for appreciating our "Southern" accents. Finally, Americans have come to embrace all the different dialects heard on our soil. Not too long ago this would have been considered a handicap.

To Rob and our other friends at Dorot Foods, we say a special thanks. Your frozen herbs are such a novel approach to getting herbs into our cooking. We appreciate that you deliver such a fine product that our readers can use in any recipe. Some people just don't have time to garden, so your product offers a nice alternative. We feel we are in good company! And to James Messer and our fine friends at Galaxy Foods, we want to thank you for believing in us enough to introduce us to Dorot Foods. What a door you opened for us, and for this we will never forget you. To Lisa Selip and everyone at Lowes Foods and other sponsors, we want to thank you for allowing us to represent your *great* products to our lovely viewers and readers. We look forward to a long and prosperous relationship.

Finally, to all our family and friends, thank you for being there during all our highs and lows (of which there have been many!). It is so nice to know that you guys are always there to offer comfort and counsel when we need it.

And last, we want to acknowledge our dear readers. In these ever-changing times in which we live, we keep seeing that there really is nothing new under the sun. The idea of going green is actually how people lived prior to our current modern era. "Green" technology only needed to be updated, so to speak. We encourage you to always think of how to live without being wasteful. When it comes to foods, stay fresh and organic. Whenever possible, try your hand at gardening. There really isn't a more rewarding endeavor than starting with a tiny seed or plant and ending up with fresh foods or herbs. Our desire is that this book will serve as a source of inspiration to you.

INTRODUCTION

There is a certain comfort one comes to feel when growing herbs. Just knowing that our ancestors grew their own food and herbs links our gardening endeavors to theirs. Ancient as well as modern-day gardeners trod the same path, preparing the soil, selecting and sowing seeds, propagating plants, and praying for sun and rain.

All gardeners have enjoyed the same benefits of growing their own food. However, an added advantage when growing your own herbs is the wonderful scent of lavender; the refreshing, cool aroma of mint; or the delicate taste of chervil…to mention a few. No matter how large or small your herb garden, foods simply taste better when prepared with fresh herbs. Yes, many culinary herbs can now be found in the fresh produce section of the supermarket. However, they pale in taste when compared with a handful of freshly picked herbs from your very own garden. For that reason, we want to share with you tips on growing herbs successfully in a garden, or potted in containers on a patio, or even placed indoors on a sunny windowsill.

Growing herbs can also be part of a green lifestyle. Stay green, get green, learn green, be green! What is all this talk about green? Seriously, isn't it about time all of mankind started paying attention to what we are doing to the environment as well as what we are putting into our bodies? We certainly think so and have thought that way for a very long time. The body has been very efficiently designed to absorb what is natural. When you ingest food that has been artificially colored or flavored, the body becomes disoriented. Blueberries are welcomed, but blueberry-flavored candy? Water is always welcomed into the body, but artificially flavored water? What do you think the stomach would rather have? Without becoming too authoritative, we ask you to think green when making food choices.

Upon reading our book, should you decide to try your hand at gardening, go as organic as possible. Follow our suggestions and stay green in your choices. You'll be glad and your body will be even happier.

In the following pages, we have chosen a number of our favorite culinary herbs, designing recipes and even whole meals around them. We have researched each herb to bring you history and lore, along with gardening and culinary information. We hope you will find the lore and cooking tips both enlightening and entertaining as you plan your garden and cultivate new tastes for your kitchen menus. Please read the information thoroughly before trying a recipe for the first time.

At the end of each chapter, we have left blank pages for you to record both your garden and kitchen findings. Perhaps you would like to try the same recipe, only using some different herbs, to create a new taste. For whatever reason you choose to use them, the blank pages are there for your convenience and your notes.

It is our sincere desire that you enjoy *The Herb Garden Gourmet: Grow Herbs, Eat Well, and Be Green*. There is so much to learn about the world of herbs! We thank you for inviting us into your cookbook collection and we hope you will refer to our book often, as you enjoy this fresh and healthy way to add flavor to your cooking.

—Tim and Jan

Chapter One

GARDENING WITH HERBS

Herbs can be planted in their very own garden, in the vegetable garden, or even in containers. Wherever you desire to plant them, rest assured they are easy to grow and will reward you quite well in the kitchen.

Most herbs are actually perennial plants, meaning they will return each year and for years to come. Herbs generally need six to eight hours of sun each day, minimal fertilizing, well-drained soil, and sometimes a little spring pruning for renewal. Winter mulching is a good idea in areas where the ground freezes. In our hot, humid Southern climate, nematodes, fungal diseases, and high heat often bother plants.

When planting annual herbs such as basil, dill, chervil, and cilantro, try planting them in a different area each year (in essence rotating your crops). Also, consider planting marigolds among the herbs to help repel nematodes from the soil. A border of marigolds around the garden edge also helps to discourage pests. For the most part, there are solutions to the cultural problems that may arise when growing herbs in your specific areas, and if you still harbor fear about growing your own herb garden, you can always grow just a few plants on a sunny kitchen windowsill.

Remember, the great majority of herbs fall into two categories: annuals, which are herbs that live only one season, and perennials, which are those herbs that live two seasons or more. By far the easiest herbs we have grown are those that come back year after year. Some of these include sage, thyme, oregano, chives, tarragon, and lavender. These popular herbs can be purchased from spring through early fall at most local nurseries. If this year will be your first attempt at trying an herb garden, we would like to suggest you start with one plant each of tarragon, thyme, oregano, and sage, two chive plants, and perhaps three or four basil plants. Maybe your experience of cooking with herbs is limited, so these tried-and-true herbs are all you will need to make an interesting change to your cooking as well as your gardening.

Start with an area four feet by six feet that gets at least 6 hours of sun a day and has good drainage. Rake the area to rid it of any clods and rocks. Spread several inches of organic matter or compost over the soil; then with a spading fork, work these enrichments into the top six inches of soil, mixing and breaking up the soil thoroughly. You want your soil to be well prepared, light and aerated, and porous.

When you are ready to plant, begin by placing the shortest herbs in the front, such as the thyme and chives. The middle area of your garden should hold the sage and the tarragon, and the taller oregano and basil should be positioned in the back. Be sure to space the plants accordingly, as the thyme and chives will each need about a foot of space for growing room, and the others about two feet of space to stretch and grow. Dig a hole about a foot across for each plant and sprinkle some additional amendments into the bottom of the hole. You can amend with manure, or compost, and then add a few tablespoons of blood meal or fishmeal as a source of nitrogen.

Carefully nudge each herb seedling out of its container; then plant into the prepared hole, making sure the crown of the plant is level with the bed. Add back surrounding soil and tamp it in place around the seedling, being careful to not compact the soil too densely, yet leaving no air pockets. Water the new plant, making sure all the roots have received a good soaking. To cut down on watering and weeding, place several inches of mulch around each plant. For the first week or so, keep the new plants moist. Then use your judgment—should the weather turn hot or windy, or if the plants start to wilt, water as needed. If weeds do come, pull them so the herbs do not have to compete for water and nutrients. (An excellent time to weed is after a good rain. Weeds "pull" more easily out of wet soil than dry, releasing their pesky root balls without disturbing surrounding plants.)

After about six weeks or so, you should be able to harvest. With herbs it seems the more you harvest, the more you have. Remember with the basil, when flower heads begin to appear, cut them back. This will encourage the plants to put out lush new leaves instead of setting seed. Chives also do well by clipping their flower heads; and the more you harvest the more chives will grow.

We know many of you simply do not have room for a formal herb garden. Perhaps you have a small yard that features a birdbath. You could border the area beneath the birdbath with an array of herbs. Maybe you have some space at the front of the house, by a porch or a walkway, or even at the edge of your yard if you live in town. Look around and see what options you have. If nothing seems workable, think about container gardening, or filling a sunny window box with your favorite herbs. Even a well-placed whisky half-barrel, or an antique wheelbarrow, or a raised bed bordered by railroad ties can provide a unique setting for a small herb garden. Wagon wheels, with their spokes, can provide a circular setting for a mini herb garden.

Chapter Two

GOOD NEIGHBORS

Planting Your Garden Wisely

Good neighbors are something we all desire, and this applies to your "gardening neighborhood" as well. How about the neighbors in your garden?

Yes, we are talking about keeping bugs away, and improving the soil and growing conditions with plants that are made to be compatible neighbors. We know that many of you are planning your gardens, poring over seed catalogs, and making your decisions as to what will go into the rows and beds you will be planting. Perhaps one of the most important things to consider is the concept of companion planting.

Beets are good companions for many of the vegetables we enjoy in our summer gardens, such as lettuce, bush beans, onions, kohlrabi, and most members of the cabbage family. Do keep away from a combination of beets and pole beans, for they do not make good neighbors. You must also keep wild mustard (or charlock) away from beets, as the mustard will slow down the development of this root vegetable.

There are many members of the cabbage family, some of which include turnips, cauliflower, collards, Brussels sprouts, and of course, cabbage to name a few. All members of this family have similar likes and dislikes when it comes to insects, feeding, and soil, as well as the neighbors they want to live near. Keep them away from pole beans, strawberries, and tomatoes. All cabbage family members are buddies with plants that are aromatic and produce many blossoms. Here is where some herbs can come into the picture. Hyssop, thyme, dill, sage, peppermint, and rosemary would love to live near members of the cabbage family. Also celery, onions, and potatoes make good companion plants as well.

Carrots are almost anyone's friends, except apples. After harvesting, be sure to keep the apples away from the carrots, as apples will cause the carrots to take on a bitter taste. The carrot fly is a nuisance to carrots and can be avoided, or at least held in check, by planting rosemary, wormwood, onions, or leeks nearby. Good vegetable neighbors for carrots include bush beans, lettuce, leeks, onions, peas, and tomatoes.

Many of us like to grow our own cucumbers, which grow close to the ground but literally look up to their good neighbors such as corn, sunflowers, beans, and peas. Corn will help prevent cucumber wilt and at the same time will help deter raccoons. Radishes planted near cucumbers will repel the cucumber beetle. When you are planting your garden, be sure to add a few radish seeds to each hill of cucumber seeds and allow the radishes to grow to maturity. It is best to keep cucumber plantings separate from potatoes and aromatic herbs.

We love lettuce and eat salads as often as possible. As experienced gardeners, we all know how much rabbits love lettuce too. Try planting some green onions amidst the lettuce to deter the rabbits and keep them at bay. Many of the vegetables that we enjoy in our salads love to grow in close proximity with garden lettuce. Radishes, cucumbers, and carrots all make good neighbors both in the garden and in the salad bowl. Lettuce also feels at home planted near strawberries.

Nothing compares to fresh peas from the garden in spring. Peas have plenty of friends and make good companion plants for carrots, turnips, cucumbers, corn, beans, and many of the aromatic herbs. However, peas will not be happy near onions, garlic, and gladiola corms.

Potatoes, and their vines, have lots of friends but also a number of adversaries. Potato vines and cucumber vines do not make good neighbors, as their close proximity to each other will lead to potato blight. The same goes for pumpkins as each will inhibit the other's growth. Tomatoes and melons should also be planted separately from potatoes. Okay, so where are these so-called friends? Try incorporating sweet corn, broccoli, cabbage, and peas. A neighbor of horseradish also makes for healthier and more disease resistant potato plants.

Perhaps the favorite of garden plants is the prized tomato. Grow tomatoes near chives, carrots, garlic, parsley, marigolds, and nasturtiums, as they make preferred neighbors. Asparagus will benefit from the tomato's ability to deter the asparagus beetle. Tomatoes are best kept away from the many members of the cabbage family, and are most unhappy if planted near potatoes and fennel.

These are just a few suggestions on how and where to place your plants within a mixed vegetable and herb garden that has a good balance of clay, silt, sand, and organic matter. Here in the southeast, most gardeners have clay-based soil. No need to despair however because clay soil has the capacity to become terrific garden soil when sufficient amounts of organic matter have been added. How do you recognize clay soil? Clay soil tends to be heavy and difficult to dig. It stays wet for a long time after heavy rains and may drain very poorly. Once it dries out, it becomes very hard... yes, that is the description of our soil.

Chapter Three

SETTING THE STAGE WITH SOIL

The great Thomas Jefferson once stated, "No occupation is so grand to me as the culture of the earth…" While we agree that the cultivation of the earth is important, we had never thought of it as grand, that is until we devoted time to improving our soil and reaping the handsome rewards.

The payback for soil amending comes in the form of easier planting, healthy results, reduced weeding, and abundant harvests. When the garden soil is in good shape, it holds more moisture during times of drought; and when the heavy rains do fall, good soil will drain faster. Before starting a new project, become familiar with basic soil properties and get to know the kind of soil in your yard and garden site. This will allow you to best know how to use your time and energy when amending your soil.

Soil is composed of four main elements: water, air, mineral matter, and organic matter. And there are basically four soil types: sand, clay, silt, and loam. Our goal is to arrive at a healthy balance for our soil type.

So what can we do to improve our soil? Digging the earth to break up the subsoil and incorporate air will result in a noticeable improvement. But this is only temporary since heavy rains will come and beat the soil back down. That leaves the addition of organic matter, fertilizer, and minerals as the way to bring improvements. If you want to turn frustrating soil into "black gold," organic matter is the best addition. Organic matter is simply decomposed plant material. When added to clay soil, it creates tiny air pockets that will aid drainage. Therefore each time you cultivate your soil, work in additional organic matter.

I can hear your next question: where can I get some organic matter or compost? Well, compost can be made from a number of sources: rotted manure, chopped leaves, cover crops, kitchen waste, straw, peat moss, rotted sawdust, and wood chips. Be sure to allow raw materials to decompose before you add them to your soil. If sawdust and wood chips are mixed into the soil before the raw materials have rotted, they will use up the nitrogen in the soil. Also fresh manure will burn the plant roots if added before it has time to rot. Experienced gardeners keep a perpetual compost pile from which to gather their soil amendments; however, there is nothing wrong with purchasing conveniently seasoned and prepared fertilizers and amendments from your local nursery or garden center.

Minerals are also an inexpensive way to amend the soil. Why not dust on some rock powders in the fall so they will have time to work into your soil before spring rolls around? They will condition the soil slowly over several months, or even years, and will bring only positive results to both your plants' and your own health. After all, we eat vegetables and fruits not only to satisfy hunger but also to put vitamins and minerals into our bodies. And yes, Virginia, minerals come from pulverized rocks. Here in western North Carolina we use a lot of lime to sweeten our acidic soil. It raises the soil's pH and increases the availability of micronutrients. Apply 1 to 10 pounds per 100 square feet.

Gypsum is another inexpensive mineral that supplies calcium to the soil as well as helping to break up compacted, heavy clay soil. How often do we hear about the need to add calcium to our diets? Listen up, gardeners, vegetables grown in soil that has minerals added to it can only benefit our bodies. Not only are we helping the soil, we are helping ourselves! Just remember that good soil takes time. By adding large amounts of organic matter and mineral amendments to the soil in one fell swoop you will certainly see a great difference, but the improvements do not stop there.

Where you cultivate and replant each year, always add organic matter. Your plants will benefit, the soil will benefit, your harvests will be more bountiful, and your health will benefit as well.

Chapter Four

CONTAINER GARDENING

Container gardening is a phrase we have heard often. So what does this mean? Container gardening is for those who do not have enough yard space to create a garden and in this instance, for this cookbook, an herb garden. So if yard space is at a premium and you really want to have an herb garden, container gardening may be just what you need to consider.

Herbs certainly look handsome in containers, whether housed in pots of lively primary colors or housed in aged terra-cotta pots for a more cottage-garden effect. Imagine a large terra-cotta pot filled with bright red and orange nasturtiums cascading down the side. Perhaps you could try your hand at sponging another terra-cotta pot a pretty soft blue, then filling it with a purple sage plant. Choosing a variety of pastel colors to sponge on several different sizes of terra-cotta pots, then filling them with the herbs of your choice could really turn into an interesting project. Before you choose your herbs, gather the pots and coat both the inside and the outside with water-based, nontoxic liquid waterproofing (which can be found at a well-stocked hardware store). Allow twenty-four hours for this to dry, then coat the interior of the pots with roofing compound or asphalt, stopping 2 inches from the pot's rim. (Again, go to the hardware or garden center to find this product.) It may seem like a lot of trouble, but if you will take the time to carry out this procedure, the pots will "do your herbs right" and last for a nice long time. Use acrylic paints when decorating the exteriors of the pots and allow your imagination to run wild. Group contrasting or complimentary pots, companioned with a variety of herbs and flowers, to create colorful and artistic additions to your patio, porch, balcony, or chosen outdoor area. Be as creative with your planting as you are with your cooking!

You will not need to limit yourself to terra-cotta pots to house your herbs. We always marvel at the variety of objects in which one can plant herbs. How about a pair of rain boots? Maybe an old roaster that is no longer fit for the kitchen. Anything you can plant in and pick up to move to another space or even indoors allows you to be a container gardener. An advantage to container gardening is the portability of your plants, as you can change your arrangement with the ever-changing sun conditions of the season, or as the plants grow and change size. Gardening seems to be a continual work in progress and will need your tender attention throughout the season.

There are several important things to remember when you plant in containers. First, look for soil mixes that have been formulated specifically for containers. This is very important, as your typical garden soil tends to be a bad choice because it drains rather poorly when "trapped" in containers. Plus garden soil is all too often filled with weed seeds. So stick to packaged soil mixes that you can find at your local garden center.

Remember that you must have a drainage hole in the bottom of your container to prevent the plant from drowning. Since this is necessary, at planting time, cover the hole with a piece of window screening or a small square of weed cloth before filling the container with soil. This serves to keep the dirt in, and the slugs and bugs out! Drainage is ever so important, because plant roots need to breathe. Remember this when using "found objects" and antique items as alternative containers instead of traditional terra-cotta pots. These items might provide added interest to your groupings, but they need drainage holes to function well.

To avoid pale plants, fertilize frequently and evenly. We always feel that organic fertilizer yields the best results, so we recommend a biweekly dose of fish emulsion. Every six weeks or so, a dose of granulated fishmeal or a slow release fertilizer will bring added, pleasant results.

Probably the most difficult aspect of container gardening is maintaining correct moisture in the soil. Herbs such as basil and chervil are considered succulent herbs, yet will suffer if they do not receive enough moisture. On the other hand, sage and rosemary will suffer root rot if given too much water. Always feel the soil. If it is dry, water it; if it is damp, stay away from it. For the most part, any kind of container plant likes to be completely dry before having another drink of water.

Please learn how to properly water your plants. All too often, even if rain has fallen, plant foliage is too large to allow much water to get into the container. Therefore, water twice when watering! The first time to moisten the soil; the second time to actually give the plant a nice drink. (An option to consider is "planting the pots" into the ground, if possible, to keep watering to a minimum.)

Make sure you place the containers near the kitchen door as the whole purpose of growing herbs in containers is to allow you to enjoy fresh herbs in your many cooking endeavors. When fall or winter closes in (timing will depend on where you live), bring the containers indoors after checking for insects that may have made a home on your plants. Prune the plants back and bring them to a shady location. Leave them there for several transitional weeks to get them used to lower light levels. Make an indoor home for them in a location that gets at least six hours of sun daily. Turn the containers every week or so in order for all sides to receive equal light. Maintain good air circulation and do not allow the plants to touch each other. By doing this you can extend your supply of fresh herbs well beyond your outdoor growing season. Chive and parsley plants are well suited for "indoor gardening." We wish you well with your herbal gardening. May all your herbal endeavors be successful!

Chapter Five

BASIL

Basil lends itself to a spicy, mildly peppery flavor with just a trace of mint and clove. The best time to use basil is in its fresh state, but frozen or dried leaves are almost as good. Chop, mince, or crush the leaves before adding to your recipes, and don't forget to eat the flowers as well.

Grow in full sun in a rich and moist soil. Shelter from cold and wind in colder weather, or move indoors as a potted plant. To extend useful plant life, pinch out flowering shoots, and root non-flowering side shoots in separate pots during summer for later use indoors.

Basil makes a great addition to the herb garden, so by all means grow some! The seeds can be sown outdoors after the ground temperature has reached 50°F. Place the seeds about 1/8 inch deep, thinning the plants 1 foot apart when the seedlings appear. Basil prefers a well-drained, rich soil, so planting with rotted manure or compost mixed in the soil is a good idea. Mulching after the seedlings have shot up is beneficial and will be of great help in times of drought.

CREAMY BACON AND MUSHROOM SAUCE WITH LINGUINE

Serves 4

- 1/2 pound bacon
- 1 cup mushrooms (quartered)
- 1 cup green onions (white part only), sliced
- 1/2 cup white wine
- 1 cup chicken stock
- 1 cup heavy cream
- 1/2 cup Parmesan cheese
- 2 tablespoons Essence (see page 15)
- 12 ounces linguine, cooked
- 1/2 cup green onions (green part), minced
- Salt and freshly ground black pepper to taste

Sauté bacon until soft brown, then remove from the pan. Save about 2 tablespoons of drippings to sauté the mushrooms and onions (white parts only) for about 2 to 3 minutes, then remove them from the pan. Deglaze with white wine and reduce by half. Add chicken stock and reduce by half again. Add heavy cream and reduce until the mixture coats the back of a spoon. Add remaining ingredients and cook for another 2 to 3 minutes. If sauce is too thin, you may need to add some fresh lemon juice to tighten. Pour sauce over the linguine. Garnish with green parts of onions. Serve and enjoy!

ESSENCE

1 tablespoon dried or 2 tablespoons fresh basil

1 tablespoon dried or 2 tablespoons fresh parsley

3 cloves garlic, minced

1 tablespoon sea salt

Work these ingredients together and use them in the recipes given or try in your own recipes. However you use this Essence, I'm sure you will be pleased with the results.

HERBAL ITALIAN DRESSING

Serves 4

2 tablespoons Essence (see page 15)

1 tablespoon mustard

$^{1}/_{3}$ cup red wine vinegar

1 cup olive oil

Pepper to taste

Add mustard, pepper, and vinegar to the Essence. While whisking this together, slowly drizzle in the olive oil until emulsified. Serve over a nice green salad.

Basil Lore

Rumor has it that the ancient Greek and Roman physicians believed that in order to achieve a good crop of basil, one had to shout and swear loudly. You can be the judge of that one!

BASIL AND GARLIC SPREAD

Serves 8

2 tablespoons Essence (see page 15)
$^1/_2$ cup unsalted butter, softened

Add the Essence to the butter and mix together thoroughly. Spread over hard crusted bread and brown in the oven. You will love this one, I'm sure!

TROPICAL FRU FRUS

Serves 6

- 1/2 cup mayonnaise
- 1 small carton cream cheese
- 1 teaspoon lemon basil leaves (optional)
- 1 head iceberg lettuce
- 1 jar maraschino cherries
- 1 can crushed pineapple
- 1/2 cup pecans in broken pieces
- 1/3 cup dried shredded coconut

Several hours before preparation time, mix the mayonnaise, cream cheese, and the basil (if available) together and chill. To prepare, wash the lettuce and tear off sections about the size of your hand. Spread the cream cheese and mayonnaise mixture over the dried lettuce sections. Top with the remaining fruits and nuts. This makes a light dessert that would be easy to serve after a great pasta meal.

Basil Trivia

Known as the king of herbs, basil gets its name from the Greek word meaning royalty. With over 150 varieties, surely every household around the world has some use for it.

GRILLED MARINATED CHICKEN

Serves 4

4 boneless, skinless chicken breasts
1 recipe Herbal Italian Dressing (see page 16)

Place dressing and chicken in a gallon-size freezer bag and squeeze out all the air. Seal and place in refrigerator for 2 hours. Take out meat and place on a medium-high-heat grill. Grill chicken 4 to 5minutes on each side. Do not overcook as the chicken will dry out.

GRILLED MARINATED BEEF

Serves 4

4 (6-ounce) steaks, any cut or style

1 cup Herbal Italian Dressing (see page 16)

Place dressing and meat in a gallon-size freezer bag and squeeze out all the air. Seal and place in refrigerator for about 2 hours. Take out meat and place on grill over medium-high heat. Grill to desired doneness. Remember that the less give there is to the meat the more cooked it will be. To get a medium-cooked steak touch the meat and if it gives a little it is cooked to perfection.

ITALIAN CHICKEN

Serves 8

8 boneless, skinless chicken breast halves
4 tomatoes, quartered
1/2 cup chopped mushrooms
1 cup Herbal Italian Dressing (see page 16)
1/2 cup chopped green onions
1/2 teaspoon dried oregano

Preheat oven to 350°F. Place chicken breasts, tomatoes, and mushrooms in a 9 x 13-inch baking dish. Combine dressing, green onion, and oregano, and pour over chicken and vegetables. Bake 1 hour to 1 hour and 15 minutes.

Cooking Tip

If you check your pantry and you find that you have run out of basil, do not despair; use oregano. If your recipe calls for 1 teaspoon of basil, you should use 1 teaspoon of oregano as a replacement.

TIM AND JAN'S MEATBALL SUPREME

Serves 4

- 1 pound ground round
- 1/2 small onion, chopped
- 1/2 small green bell pepper, chopped
- 1/8 teaspoon freshly ground black pepper
- 1/4 cup cornmeal
- 1 teaspoon salt
- 1 teaspoon dried basil
- 1 1/2 teaspoons dry mustard
- 2 teaspoons chili powder
- 1/4 cup water
- 1 egg, slightly beaten
- 1/4 cup all-purpose flour
- 2 to 4 tablespoons cold pressed olive oil
- 2 (8-ounce) cans tomato sauce
- 1 cup water
- 2 teaspoons Worcestershire sauce
- 3 large potatoes, quartered
- 1 pound carrots, sliced in strips
- 2 large onions, quartered

Combine first 11 ingredients. Mix and form into 12 to 14 meatballs. Roll in flour. Brown in hot olive oil. Remove and set aside. Add tomato sauce, water and Worcestershire to pan drippings. Stir and bring to a boil. Remove from heat.

Preheat oven to 350°F. Layer meatballs and vegetables in a deep 4-quart casserole dish. Pour sauce over all and bake covered for about 1 hour. Carrots should still be crisp. Serve and enjoy.

TOMATO BISQUE

Serves 4

1/4 cup butter
1/2 cup minced onion
1/2 cup all-purpose flour
1 1/2 cups milk
1 cup chicken stock
2 (14 1/2 -ounce) cans Italian plum tomatoes, juice reserved
1 tablespoon honey
2 tablespoons minced parsley
1 teaspoon dill weed
1 teaspoon dried basil
1/4 teaspoon dried marjoram
1 bay leaf
Salt and freshly ground black pepper to taste

Melt butter in pan. Add onions and sauté until transparent. Lower heat. Add flour and cook, stirring constantly. Add milk and chicken stock. Whisk until smooth and thick. Puree tomatoes in blender. Add puree, including juice, to sauce mixture and mix. Add remaining ingredients and simmer for 45 minutes, stirring frequently. Remember to remove bay leaf before serving.

ASIAN GRILLED CHICKEN

Serves 4

4 boneless, skinless chicken breasts
1/2 cup teriyaki sauce
1/4 cup soy sauce
3 tablespoons white vinegar
2 tablespoons dried basil
1 tablespoon dried parsley
1 teaspoon sesame oil
2 cloves garlic, minced
Freshly ground black pepper to taste

Mix all ingredients together in a gallon-size freezer bag. Squeeze to remove all the air from the bag and seal it up. Place in refrigerator for about 2 hours.

Take meat out of refrigerator and place on grill over medium-high heat. Grill 4 to 5 minutes on each side until done. Do not overcook as the chicken will become dried out.

NOTES FROM THE KITCHEN

NOTES FROM THE GARDEN

Chapter Six

DILL

There is nothing as good as dill pickles made from fresh homegrown dill, garlic, and cucumbers!

That is typically how most of us think of dill. However, dill leaves combine well with many foods because the leaves contain just two distinctively flavored oils. These two oils have the familiar taste of celery and lemon, so it is no wonder dill harmonizes with, rather than overwhelms, many foods.

Dill is a native to the Mediterranean and southern Russia, but tends to be at home anywhere in the world.

To grow dill in your herb garden, locate a space that gets at least six hours of sun per day. Sow seeds once the soil has warmed or use transplants from a garden center. Dill tends to spread out, so plant it at least 2 feet away from other plants. In case of drought, water often. Otherwise, allow nature to do the watering.

Both the leaves and the seeds can be used for cooking and medicinal purposes. The best dill to use for cooking is fresh, so if you enjoy cooking with dill, then be sure to grow some!

We recommend using fresh dill to host a summer clambake. You'll find the recipes needed to do so in this chapter.

SUMMER CLAMBAKE OR CLAMSTEAM

Serves 8–10

2 cups fish stock
4 sprigs of fresh dill
1 can of your favorite beer
1 tablespoon unsalted butter
1 teaspoon kosher salt
12 lobster tails
3 pounds small white onions, peeled
12 ears of corn, unshucked
3 pounds red potatoes, washed
4 pounds steamer clams, washed

Prepare pit for clambake in the traditional manner, or use a multipurpose outdoor cooker to prepare the food. We use an outdoor cooker, fueled by a propane burner provided by the manufacturer. Place the stock, dill, beer, butter, and salt in the bottom of the stockpot. Add the lobster tails, followed by the onions, corn, potatoes, and clams. Cover the pot and place on the stand. Follow the manufacturer's directions to bring the food to a boiling point. Allow about 30 minutes for the food to cook thoroughly, and check to be sure the potatoes are fork tender. Remove the pot from the heat source; place the food on large platters. Serve and enjoy!

DILL BUTTER WITH GARLIC

Serves 8

2 cups melted butter (not margarine)
4 cloves minced garlic
1/4 cup chopped fresh dill

Add garlic and dill to the butter. Mix until well combined. You can use this spread on hard crusted bread. Just remember to toast it under your broiler right before serving. You can also melt this butter and use it as a dip for steamed shrimp or crab. Add your own creative touch by trying other fresh herbs with this butter. For example, chives would be a wonderful addition.

LADYBUG DILLY SALAD

Serves 4

Assortment of mixed baby greens (use your favorite)

1 (8-ounce) can sliced beets, drained

2 ounces fresh pea pods, trimmed (1 cup)

1 small red onion, chopped

1/4 cup cracked black pepper

1 sprig fresh dill

1 recipe Red Wine Vinaigrette (see page 31)

To assemble: Line salad plates with assorted greens. Arrange beets, pea pods, and onions atop greens. Sprinkle with black pepper; then pour prepared dressing over top.

Cooking Tip

It is easy to swap out fresh herbs for dried herbs. If your recipe calls for 1 teaspoon of dried herbs, then just use about 1 tablespoon of your fresh herbs. Just keep in mind that dried herbs are more concentrated in flavor than fresh, but nothing beats the taste of fresh herbs you grew yourself.

RED WINE VINAIGRETTE

Serves 4

1/2 cup olive oil

1/2 cup red wine vinegar

2 tablespoons burgundy or dry red wine

2 teaspoons sugar

2 teaspoons snipped fresh thyme or 1/2 teaspoon dried crushed thyme

2 teaspoons snipped fresh savory or 1/2 teaspoon dried crushed savory

1/2 teaspoon kosher salt

1/2 teaspoon prepared mustard

Combine ingredients in a screw-top jar. Cover and shake well. Store in refrigerator for up to two weeks. Shake well before using. For a refreshing dessert, we recommend this vinaigrette over an icy combination of fruits. Give this easy suggestion a try after your clambake.

STRAWBERRY-KIWI ICE

Serves 4

4 cups sliced strawberries or one package frozen berries
1 1/4 cups cherry juice, unsweetened
3/4 cup sugar
2 cups sliced fresh kiwi
Champagne or ginger ale (optional)
Fresh mint sprigs for garnish

Stir together the strawberries, 1/2 cup of the cherry juice, and the sugar in a medium saucepan. Bring to boil; reduce heat. Cover and simmer for 3 to 5 minutes or until strawberries are tender and sugar is dissolved. Remove from heat and add the remaining juice and kiwis. Allow to cool to room temperature. Pour the cooled mixture into a blender container or a food processor bowl and blend or process until smooth. Transfer mixture to a 9 x 9 x 2-inch nonmetal freezer container. Cover and freeze for 4 to 5 hours or until almost firm. While this is freezing, chill another large bowl in the refrigerator or freezer. Remove the frozen mixture and break into small chunks. In the chilled bowl, beat the chunks with an electric mixer on medium speed until smooth but not melted. Return mixture to the freezer container. Cover and place in the freezer again for at least 6 hours more, or until firm.

To serve, use a melon baller or a small ice cream scoop to scrape the surface of the ice and shape into small balls. Spoon 4 or 5 balls into each dessert dish. Garnish with champagne or ginger ale and a sprig of mint.

DILLED POTATO SALAD

Serves 8

3 pounds red or yellow potatoes
6 eggs, hardboiled
1 (8-ounce) carton sour cream
1/4 cup mayonnaise
1 tablespoon fresh dill, chopped
1 tablespoon fresh parsley, chopped
1 teaspoon prepared mustard
1/2 teaspoon salt
1/2 teaspoon freshly ground black pepper

Boil and cool potatoes; then dice. Place in a glass dish. Peel eggs then dice. Add to the potatoes. In a separate bowl, add the rest of the ingredients and mix thoroughly. Pour over the potatoes and eggs and again mix thoroughly. Cover and chill several hours. Garnish with additional dill if desired.

HAM AND CHEESE OMELET WITH DILL

Serves 4

6 eggs, slightly beaten
1/4 cup milk
1/4 teaspoon curry
1 teaspoon dried dill
Cooking spray
1/2 cup onion, minced
1/2 cup red pepper, chopped
1/2 cup green pepper, chopped
2/3 cup cooked ham, chopped
1/2 cup shredded cheddar cheese
1/4 cup shredded Havarti cheese

Combine the first four ingredients. Set aside. Coat a 10-inch omelet pan or skillet with cooking spray. Sauté onions and peppers in omelet pan over medium heat until tender. Add egg mixture and as the mixture starts to cook, use a spatula to gently lift the edges of the omelet. Tilt the pan so the uncooked portion will flow beneath the omelet. Place the chopped ham and cheeses over the omelet. At this point, cover the pan and allow the omelet to cook about 3 more minutes or until it is set. Again use the spatula to fold the omelet in half. Serve immediately.

DILLY BREAD

Serves 6

1/2 cup unsalted butter
1 teaspoon sea salt
3 cloves garlic, minced
1/4 cup finely chopped fresh dill
1/4 cup finely chopped fresh thyme
1 loaf sourdough or other good quality bread, sliced
1/4 cup grated Parmesan cheese

Preheat broiler. Soften butter and add salt, garlic, dill, and thyme. Mix thoroughly and spread over bread slices. Top with Parmesan cheese. Place under the broiler until butter has melted and turned golden. Serve immediately.

FRESH TOMATO SOUP WITH DILL

Serves 4

2 tablespoons unsalted butter
2 medium onions, finely chopped
3 cloves garlic, minced
1 large carrot, peeled and finely chopped
3 cups chicken broth
15 fresh, ripe tomatoes, seeded and chopped
1/2 teaspoon salt
1/2 teaspoon freshly ground black pepper
1 cup half-and-half
Chopped fresh dill

Over medium heat, melt butter in a Dutch oven. Stir in the onions, garlic, and carrot, and cook until tender. Pour in the chicken broth and add the remaining ingredients except the half-and-half and the dill. Continue cooking over medium heat, uncovered, about 30 minutes, stirring occasionally. Cool slightly. In a food processor, purée the soup mixture until smooth. Return to pot and stir in half-and-half. Keep the soup warm until ready to serve. Do not boil once cream has been added. Garnish with chopped fresh dill.

DILLY DIP

Serves 6

$^1/_2$ cup sour cream
$^1/_2$ cup cottage cheese (small curd)
1 tablespoon finely chopped green pepper
1 clove garlic, minced
1 tablespoon dried dill
2 tablespoons mayonnaise
$^1/_2$ teaspoon balsamic vinegar

Mix all ingredients together. Cover and allow the flavors to blend in the refrigerator for at least one hour. Serve with a variety of vegetables for dipping.

Household Hint

If someone spills wine on your tablecloth during your meal, try this quick fix: pour salt directly on the stain and let it stay until the table has been cleared. Then treat the stain with your favorite stain remover and launder immediately.

DILLED VEGETABLES

Serves 4

1/2 medium cauliflower
1/2 pound green beans, washed, ends removed
1 yellow squash, chopped in bite-size pieces
1 zucchini, chopped in bite-size pieces
1 small red onion, sliced and separated into rings
1/2 cup bottled Italian dressing
1 teaspoon apple cider vinegar
2 teaspoons dried dill
1/2 teaspoon red pepper flakes

Remove outer leaves and stalk from the cauliflower. Check for discoloration, wash, and separate into flowerets. Leave the beans whole after trimming. Place beans and cauliflower in salted boiling water (1/2 teaspoon salt to 1 cup water). Cover and simmer about 8 minutes and drain. Place cauliflower, beans, squash, zucchini, and onion in a shallow glass dish. Place the remaining ingredients in a tightly covered container and shake to combine. Pour this mixture over the vegetables, stir gently. Cover and chill in refrigerator about 4 hours. Drain before serving. Keep unused portion in refrigerator.

SOUR CREAM AND DILL SAUCE

Serves 8

3 tablespoons unsalted butter

3 tablespoons all-purpose flour

$1\frac{1}{2}$ cups beef broth

2 teaspoons dried dill or $1\frac{1}{2}$ tablespoons chopped fresh

$\frac{1}{2}$ teaspoon salt

$\frac{1}{4}$ teaspoon ground nutmeg

$\frac{3}{4}$ cup dairy sour cream at room temperature

Melt butter in a heavy saucepan over low heat. Gradually stir in flour, cooking and stirring until bubbly. Add broth, dill, salt, and nutmeg. Remove from heat and stir in sour cream. Pour sauce over meatballs (as on page 22) and serve.

ELEGANT SALMON MOUSSE

Serves 4

1 (15½ ounce) can salmon, drained and flaked
1 medium stalk celery, chopped
1 small onion, chopped
2 cloves garlic, chopped
1½ cups half-and-half
2 tablespoons freshly squeezed lemon juice
1 teaspoon instant chicken bouillon
1 teaspoon dried dill weed
½ teaspoon salt
2 envelopes unflavored gelatin
½ cup cold water
Baguette slices for garnish

Place salmon, celery, onion, garlic, 1 cup of the half-and-half, lemon juice, bouillon, dill, and salt in a blender container. Cover and blend on high speed until smooth, about 2 minutes. Place the gelatin and the water in a heavy saucepan. Stir in remaining half-and-half. Cook over low heat, stirring constantly until gelatin is dissolved. Remove from heat and allow to cool.

Mix gelatin mixture into salmon mixture. Pour into a lightly oiled 4-cup mold. Place in refrigerator and chill for 2 hours, or until firm. Unmold onto a serving plate. Serve with lightly toasted baguette slices.

DILLED BARLEY SOUP WITH VEGETABLES

Serves 6

$2\frac{1}{2}$ cups fresh mushrooms, sliced
1 cup onion, chopped
1 medium carrot, coarsely chopped
1 celery stalk, chopped
4 cloves garlic, minced
4 tablespoons fresh dill, chopped
1 (15-ounce) can red beans
1 (15-ounce) can white beans
1 (10-ounce) package whole kernel corn
$\frac{2}{3}$ cup medium pearl barley
1 ($14\frac{1}{2}$-ounce) can stewed tomatoes, undrained
6 cups chicken stock
Salt and freshly ground black pepper, to taste

Place the mushrooms, onion, carrot, celery, and garlic in a heavy saucepan. Add herbs, beans, corn, barley, and tomatoes. Stir. Pour chicken stock into pot and cover. Simmer gently for several hours.

When making stews and soups, the longer the flavors are together, the better the dish will taste. Serve with hard crusted bread.

NOTES FROM THE KITCHEN

NOTES FROM THE GARDEN

Chapter Seven

OREGANO

For centuries people have enjoyed the wonderful taste of oregano. Although oregano is native to the Mediterranean hillsides, it is quite at home in North America from Ontario and Quebec, south to North Carolina and beyond, and west to California and Oregon.

Oregano makes a great ground cover. I raise my oregano in a space designated just for it, as it will spread wide and far with its great root system. Away from my formal herb garden, it is allowed to grow and spread freely. As with all my herbs, I gather the oregano in the morning after the dew has dried off the plants. After further drying the herbs, I place them in jars to use later in the year or to give to friends who haven't taken to growing herbs just yet.

Because oregano's peppery-thyme flavor blends well with many foods, it is a most versatile herb. It often deepens the flavor of sauces and soups by neither losing its own flavor nor overpowering others. By all means use oregano in tomato sauce for pasta or pizza. Also include the leaves in salads, butters, vinegars, or marinades.

Oregano will complement the flavor of cheese and egg dishes as well. And beef, pork, poultry, game, eggplant, beans, and summer-squash dishes will all benefit from its flavorful addition.

CHICKEN (OR VEAL) PARMESAN

Serves 6

1 pound very thin chicken (or veal) cutlets
2 large onions, minced
3 cloves garlic, minced
6 tablespoons olive oil, divided
2 (16-ounce) cans tomatoes
1 teaspoon salt
1/2 teaspoon freshly ground black pepper
1 (8-ounce) can tomato sauce
1 (6-ounce) can tomato paste
2 tablespoons oregano
2 tablespoons basil
1 teaspoon fennel seeds
1/4 cup dried breadcrumbs
1 1/4 cups Parmesan cheese
1 egg, beaten
1/2 pound mozzarella cheese

Preheat oven to 375°F. Cut the meat into serving pieces; set aside. Cook onions and garlic together in 3 tablespoons of the olive oil, about 5 minutes. Break the tomatoes with a fork, then add them along with the salt and pepper to the onions and garlic. Simmer about 5 minutes; then add tomato sauce, tomato paste, and herbs. Cover and simmer about 20 minutes.

Combine the breadcrumbs with 1 1/4 cups Parmesan cheese in another bowl, while sauce is simmering. Dip the cut meat into the beaten egg, then dredge through the crumb mixture. Brown in 3 tablespoons of olive oil. Transfer the meat into a shallow baking dish. Pour on 2/3 of the sauce, top with mozzarella cheese, then remaining sauce. Sprinkle with Parmesan cheese. Bake for 30 minutes. Serve with your favorite pasta. Add a nice salad of varied greens to complement the meal. Use the recipe for the Herbal Italian Salad Dressing given in the chapter on basil (see page 16).

Oregano Lore

According to folklore, in ancient Greece and Rome, brides and grooms wore wreaths of oregano (or marjoram) to symbolize the joy of their union.

ROMAINE AND RADICCHIO ITALIAN SALAD

Serves 4

Dressing

- 2 tablespoons Essence (see page 15)
- 1 tablespoon mustard
- 1/3 cup red wine vinegar
- Freshly ground black pepper to taste
- 1 cup olive oil

Mix all ingredients together except for oil until thoroughly mixed. Slowly add olive oil to the mixture while whisking until it becomes emulsified.

Greens

- 2 cups each romaine and radicchio, washed and torn into bite-size pieces
- 1/2 cup thinly sliced red onion
- 1/2 cup cherry tomatoes
- 1/4 cup fresh oregano
- 1/4 cup pitted black olives

Combine ingredients and toss with dressing. This salad combined with a pasta dish of your choice will feel so "at home" in your mouth! Be sure to include some hard crusted bread along with your meal. You'll be glad you did. After enjoying such a fine combination, you may think there is no room for dessert. However, Snow Cream, a simple dish, is just what you might need to end with (See Snow Cream, page 112).

SWEDISH MEATBALLS

Serves 8

1 pound lean ground beef
1 pound ground pork
$^1/_2$ cup seasoned breadcrumbs
$^1/_3$ cup onion, finely chopped
$^1/_4$ cup half-and-half
2 eggs, slightly beaten
4 tablespoons chopped fresh parsley, or 2 tablespoons dried
2 tablespoons chopped fresh oregano, or 1 tablespoon dried
1 teaspoon salt
1 teaspoon Worcestershire sauce
$^1/_2$ teaspoon grated lemon peel
$^1/_4$ teaspoon ground allspice

Preheat oven to 375°F. Mix all ingredients and shape into 1-inch balls. Place on the rack of a broiler pan. Bake until brown, 20 to 25 minutes. Keep warm while making the Sour Cream and Dill Sauce (see page 39).

ITALIAN FISH STEW

Serves 4

- 1/4 cup olive oil
- 1 medium onion, chopped
- 1 small green pepper, seeded and chopped
- 1 small red pepper, seeded and chopped
- 4 cloves garlic, minced
- 1 (28-ounce) can Italian tomatoes
- 1 cup chicken stock
- 1 cup dry white wine
- 2 cups potatoes, peeled and diced
- 1 teaspoon salt
- 1/2 teaspoon freshly ground black pepper
- 1 teaspoon dried oregano, crushed
- 1 teaspoon dried basil, crushed
- 1 teaspoon dried thyme, crushed
- 2 pounds fresh or frozen fish (cod or haddock), cut into 2-inch chunks
- Parmesan cheese, grated
- Fresh parsley, chopped

Heat oil in Dutch oven and sauté onions, peppers, and garlic until tender. Use a fork to slightly mash the tomatoes. Add the tomatoes to the vegetables. Stir in the stock, wine, potatoes, and the remaining seasonings. Cover and simmer for 30 minutes. Add fish and simmer another 10 minutes, or until the fish flakes easily. Serve stew in soup bowls. Sprinkle Parmesan cheese and parsley over the stew.

SHRIMP IN TOMATO CREAM SAUCE

Serves 4

4 cloves garlic, peeled and minced (or pressed for stronger flavor)
3 shallots, minced
6 Roma tomatoes (or 3 medium tomatoes), chopped
1/4 cup Lambrusco (sweet red wine)
1 small (8-ounce) can tomato sauce
1/2 teaspoon oregano (crushed to release flavor)
1/4 teaspoon basil
1 cup heavy cream
1 dozen fresh, raw, peeled jumbo shrimp
Salt and freshly ground black pepper to taste
Angel hair pasta, cooked al dente
Parsley for garnish (optional)

Sauté garlic and shallots in a little olive oil until translucent. Add chopped tomatoes and simmer about 5 minutes. Add wine and reduce sauce slightly. Add tomato sauce, oregano, and basil; cook about 10 minutes to let flavors blend. Add heavy cream and reduce to thick consistency. Just before pasta is done, add shrimp to cream sauce and cook only until shrimp turn pink throughout. Do not overcook or the shrimp will be tough. Remove shrimp and sauce immediately from heat and serve over angel hair pasta. Garnish with fresh parsley if desired.

TIM AND JAN'S CAJUN SPICE MIX

$^{1}/_{2}$ cup chili powder

$^{1}/_{2}$ cup paprika

$^{1}/_{4}$ pound kosher salt

2 tablespoons onion powder

2 tablespoons coarsely ground black pepper

2 tablespoons dried basil

2 tablespoons dried oregano

2 tablespoons ground coriander

$1^{1}/_{2}$ tablespoons dried thyme

$^{3}/_{4}$ teaspoon cayenne pepper

$^{1}/_{3}$ teaspoon cumin

Mix all ingredients together and place in a covered jar for storage. Store in a cool, dark place up to 4 months. Use this mixture for barbecue ribs, chicken, blackened fish, cajun soups or sauces, blackened steaks, and blackened pastas.

OLIVE PASTE

Makes 1 Cup

1 cup kalamata or mixed green and black olives
1 medium onion, chopped
3 tablespoons capers, rinsed
1 tablespoon chopped fresh oregano or $1\frac{1}{2}$ teaspoons dried
3 tablespoons olive oil
2 tablespoons red wine vinegar
Grated peel (no white attached) of 1 lemon
$\frac{1}{2}$ teaspoon freshly ground black pepper, or to taste

---

Place the olives in a colander and rinse very well under cold running water. Remove the pits from the olives and discard. In the bowl of a food processor, combine the pitted olives, onion, capers, oregano, olive oil, vinegar, and lemon peel. Process to a spreadable consistency. Season to taste with the pepper and store in a small covered jar in the refrigerator. Will last up to 6 months and is great on French bread and in pasta. Makes a great spread for your next party.

HEARD IT THROUGH THE GRAPEVINE

Serves 4

4 cups red or white seedless grapes

$^1/_2$ cup raisins that have been soaked overnight in white wine

1 tablespoon sugar

For something light and sweet after a heavy meal you can try this recipe. Just mix together all the ingredients. Serve in your favorite stemware. Remember that dessert does not have to be complicated to be spectacular.

NOTES FROM THE KITCHEN

NOTES FROM THE GARDEN

Chapter Eight

CORIANDER

So, which is it, coriander or cilantro? When referring to the seeds of the plant, use the term coriander, making it a spice. However, when using the leaves of the plant, it becomes an herb known as cilantro.

Whichever way you use cilantro, know that you are in good company, for this is one of the most popular herbs in the world.

Coriander seed combines the flavor of sage with a tangy citrus taste, making it a favorite in cuisines of Southeast Asia, China, Mexico, East India, South America, Spain, Central Africa, and America.

Cilantro grows comfortably in the cool months of spring and summer. One way to prolong the growing season for cilantro is to mulch around the plant so as to cool the soil. Also, pinch the flower stalk as soon as it appears, to promote leafy growth.

The following recipes are good ways to make use of your cilantro. Give them a try when cilantro is growing at its peak in your herb garden!

SOUTH OF THE BORDER DEVILED EGGS

Serves 4

12 hardboiled eggs, peeled
2/3 cup mayonnaise
1 jalapeno pepper, seeded and finely chopped
2 tablespoons ground cumin
2 tablespoons prepared mustard
2 tablespoons finely chopped cilantro
1/2 teaspoon salt
Chili powder
Additional cilantro, chopped
Finely chopped capers

Cut the eggs in half lengthwise. Remove the yolks and mash them with a fork. Stir in remaining ingredients, except the chili powder. Fill the egg halves with the yolk mixture, mounding in an attractive form. Sprinkle with the chili powder, additional cilantro, and capers. Refrigerate until serving time.

SMASHED-UP BEANS

Serves 4

1 medium onion, finely chopped
2 jalapeno peppers, seeded and finely chopped
3 cloves garlic, minced
1 teaspoon olive oil
2 cans pinto beans, rinsed and drained
1/2 cup beef broth
1 small can tomato sauce
2 tablespoons red wine vinegar
1 teaspoon dried oregano
1 teaspoon dried cilantro
1/2 teaspoon ground cumin
Salt and freshly ground black pepper to taste
Fresh cilantro, chopped, for garnish (optional)

Sauté the onion, peppers, and garlic in the olive oil over medium heat in a Dutch oven until vegetables are soft, about 5 minutes. Stir in remaining ingredients and bring to a boil. Reduce heat and simmer, uncovered, for about 10 minutes. With a potato masher, mash most of the bean mixture, leaving some of the beans whole. Garnish with additional cilantro if desired.

CHICKEN AND CILANTRO STUFFED PEPPERS

Serves 4

4 large bell peppers (use any color)
3 cups cooked chicken, finely shredded
1 (12-ounce) package frozen corn, defrosted
2/3 cup soft breadcrumbs
1 medium onion, chopped
1 (4.5-ounce) can chopped green chiles, drained
1/2 package taco seasoning
2 tablespoons chopped cilantro
Salt and freshly ground black pepper, to taste
1 (8-ounce) package shredded Monterey Jack cheese, divided
Fresh cilantro, chopped, for garnish (optional)

Preheat broiler. Cut peppers in half, and place on a lightly oiled baking sheet, cut side down. Be sure to remove the seeds and leave the stems intact. Broil 6 inches from heat source, about 5 minutes. When the peppers begin to blister, remove from oven and allow to cool as you prepare the filling. Preheat oven to 375°F.

Combine remaining ingredients with half of the cheese. Fill the peppers evenly with the mixture. Bake for 25 minutes, then remove from oven and sprinkle remaining cheese over the peppers. Return to oven and bake an additional 5 minutes, or until cheese has melted. Garnish with additional chopped cilantro if desired.

GREEN APPLE SALSA

Serves 4

2 green apples, peeled, cored, and chopped
1 cup golden raisins
1/2 cup chopped red onion
1/2 cup seeded and diced fresh poblano chiles
1/4 cup apple juice
2 tablespoons freshly squeezed lime juice
1 tablespoon rice wine vinegar
1 teaspoon fresh oregano, minced
1 teaspoon fresh cilantro, minced
Salt and freshly ground black pepper, to taste

Combine all ingredients, mixing well. Chill. Serve with pork or salmon. Can also be served warm.

CHINESE PASTA

Serves 4

- 1 (8-ounce) package fusilli pasta
- 3 tablespoons soy sauce
- 1 tablespoon plum sauce
- 1 teaspoon sesame oil
- 1/2 teaspoon red chili paste
- 1 tablespoon olive oil
- 1 red or green pepper, seeded and chopped
- 1 small onion, chopped
- 1 (12-ounce) package frozen peeled and deveined shrimp, defrosted
- 4 cloves garlic
- 1 teaspoon fresh ginger, grated
- 1/2 teaspoon freshly ground black pepper
- 2 tablespoons fresh cilantro, chopped
- 1 cup snow pea pods, cleaned and trimmed
- 2 teaspoons sesame seeds, toasted
- 3 green onions, bias-cut into 1-inch pieces

Cook fusilli according to directions. Drain. Set aside. Make the sauce by stirring together the soy sauce, plum sauce, sesame oil, and chili paste. Set aside. Heat olive oil in a large skillet or wok. Cook and stir pepper and onion for about 5 minutes. Push aside and add shrimp, garlic, ginger, pepper, and cilantro. Cook and stir another 5 minutes. Add prepared sauce and pea pods. Stir until combined and add pasta. Heat through and serve garnished with sesame seeds and green onions.

SPANISH-STYLE SHRIMP COCKTAIL

Serves 4

24 fresh or frozen raw medium shrimp
1 cup water
Juice of 2 limes
2 cloves garlic, finely minced
2 teaspoons salt
$^{1}/_{4}$ teaspoon freshly ground pepper
$^{1}/_{2}$ cup chopped tomato
1 small avocado, chopped
2 jalapeno peppers, seeded and finely minced
2 tablespoons chopped red onion
1 tablespoon chopped Italian parsley
2 tablespoons chopped fresh cilantro
2 tablespoons olive oil
$1^{1}/_{2}$ cups finely shredded lettuce
Lemon wedges

Peel the shrimp by making a shallow cut lengthwise down the back of each shrimp; wash out the sand vein. (If using frozen shrimp, do not thaw. Instead peel under cold running water.) Bring water, lime juice, garlic, salt, and pepper to a boil in a 4-quart Dutch oven. Simmer uncovered until liquid has been reduced to $^{2}/_{3}$ cup. Add shrimp. Cover and simmer 3 minutes, keeping watch that the shrimp do not overcook. Using a slotted spoon, remove the shrimp and place in a bowl of ice water. Continue to simmer the liquid left in the pot, reducing to 2 tablespoons. Drain the shrimp from the ice water and place in a glass bowl. Add the remaining 2 tablespoons of liquid to the shrimp. Add the tomato, avocado, peppers, onion, parsley, cilantro, and olive oil. Cover and place in the refrigerator for at least an hour.

To serve; place about $^{1}/_{3}$ cup of lettuce in each of 4 dishes. Divide the shrimp mixture among the dishes and garnish with lemon wedges.

MEXICAN PIZZA

Serves 4

1 package sourdough baguettes
2 to 3 cups grated sharp cheddar cheese
1 cup black olives, chopped
1 small can diced green chilies
3 green onions, chopped
1 small can tomato sauce
2 tablespoons olive oil
2 cloves garlic, minced
3 tablespoons cilantro, chopped

Preheat oven to 350ºF. Slice baguettes into 1/2-inch-thick slices. Combine all other ingredients and spread over bread. Place on cookie sheet and bake 8 to 10 minutes or until cheese has melted.

SPICY BLACK BEANS

Serves 4

2 cups dry black beans
1 cup chopped onion
1 cup chopped celery
1 medium yellow pepper, chopped and seeded
1 medium green pepper, chopped and seeded
1/2 cup chopped carrot
6 cloves garlic, minced
2 jalapeno or serrano peppers, seeded and chopped
1 tablespoon ground cumin
1 tablespoon cilantro, chopped
2 teaspoons thyme, chopped
1/2 teaspoon salt
1/2 teaspoon freshly ground black pepper
6 cups chicken stock
Fresh cilantro for garnish (optional)

Wash and sort beans. Place in heavy saucepan and cover with water. Cook rapidly for 20 minutes, then remove from heat and allow to sit overnight. Drain and return beans to the pot. Place vegetables and herbs in the pot and pour chicken stock over. Cover and allow to simmer for 2 hours or until beans are soft. Mash lightly with a potato masher. Serve over cooked rice. Garnish with fresh cilantro if desired.

AVOCADO CREAM DIP

Serves 4

3 large avocados, halved, pitted, separated from peel
Zest and freshly squeezed juice of 2 limes
2 green onions, minced
2 cloves garlic, minced
1 small can green chiles, minced
3 tablespoons minced fresh cilantro
3 tablespoons minced fresh flat-leaf parsley
$^{1}/_{2}$ cup sour cream

Put the avocado and lime juice in a bowl and mash with a masher or fork until smooth. The lime juice is to keep the avocado from turning brown. Add remaining ingredients except for sour cream and mix well. Fold in sour cream and blend until very smooth. Refrigerate for 2 hours before serving. Serve with your favorite chips.

GRILLED PORK WITH CORIANDER CHUTNEY

Serves 4–6

4 to 6 loin pork chops
Salt and freshly ground black pepper to taste
1 cup washed and packed fresh coriander leaves
4 scallions, chopped
2 cloves garlic, minced
2 tablespoons white vinegar
3 tablespoons unsalted raw pumpkin or sunflower seeds
1 tablespoon olive oil
Salt and freshly ground black pepper, to taste

Preheat grill or broiler. Salt and pepper the pork chops and grill until the internal temperature reaches 165°F. Prepare the chutney while the chops are cooking by combining remaining ingredients in food processor or a blender. Whirl gently until you have a coarse paste. Serve at once, as it will tend to separate. You could also use this to spice up the flavor of a bland soup.

Cooking Tip
Never add an ingredient that does not impart flavor.

CHICKEN CILANTRO

Serves 4

2 tablespoons freshly squeezed lime juice
1 teaspoon honey
2 tablespoons olive oil
4 boneless, skinless chicken breasts
1 cup finely crushed blue-corn tortilla chips
1 (16-ounce) jar salsa
2 tablespoons freshly minced parsley
2 tablespoons freshly minced cilantro
1/2 cup Monterey Jack cheese, shredded

Preheat oven to 350°F. Combine lime juice, honey, and olive oil in a small bowl. Wash and pat dry the chicken. Dip each breast in the lime juice mixture, then coat with crushed tortilla chips. Place coated chicken in an ungreased shallow baking dish. Bake, uncovered, for 30 minutes. Combine the herbs with the salsa and pour over chicken breasts. Sprinkle Monterey Jack cheese on top. Return to oven for an additional 5 minutes, or until cheese is melted.

CUCUMBER LIME SALSA

Serves 4

1 large cucumber, peeled, seeded, and minced
4 spring onions, sliced thinly
1 jalapeno pepper, seeded and minced
3 cloves garlic, minced
2 tablespoons freshly minced parsley
2 tablespoons freshly squeezed lime juice
2 tablespoons olive oil
2 tablespoons freshly minced cilantro
1 teaspoon cumin
1 teaspoon grated lime peel
1/2 teaspoon salt
1/4 teaspoon freshly ground pepper

This salsa recipe tastes great over Chicken Cilantro (see recipe on page 67), or may be used as a dip with chips! Mix all ingredients together in a bowl. Allow to refrigerate overnight. Stir again and serve.

RICE AND BEANS WITH VINAIGRETTE

Serves 4

2 cups cooked long grain rice
1 (16-ounce) can black beans, rinsed and drained
1/2 cup red bell pepper, seeded and chopped
1/2 cup green bell pepper, seeded and chopped
1 tablespoon chopped jalapeno pepper
2 tablespoons chopped parsley
2 tablespoons chopped cilantro
3 tablespoons olive oil
2 tablespoons red wine vinegar
2 tablespoons water
1 teaspoon ground cumin
1/2 teaspoon salt, or to taste
1/2 teaspoon freshly ground black pepper, or to taste

Combine rice, beans, peppers, parsley, and cilantro. Use a jar with a tight-fitting lid to combine the remaining ingredients. Shake well and let set for several hours. Pour over the rice-bean mixture, tossing to coat. Refrigerate until serving time.

BLUEBERRY CRISP

Serves 6

1/4 cup unbleached all-purpose flour
3 tablespoons unsalted butter, cut into 1/8-inch cubes
1/2 cup sugar
2 tablespoons firmly packed brown sugar
1 teaspoon lightly crushed coriander seeds
3 cups fresh or frozen blueberries
Zest of one lemon, yellow part only
2 tablespoons sugar for sprinkling
Whipped cream or ice cream for topping

Preheat oven to 375°F. Butter a 1 1/2-quart baking dish; set aside. In a food processor, combine flour, butter, and both of the sugars. Pulse gently until mixture resembles cornmeal. Stir in the coriander. In buttered baking dish, combine blueberries, lemon zest, and sugar. Sprinkle flour mixture over the top. Bake 45 minutes, or until the topping has reached a nice golden brown. Serve warm with a dollop of whipped cream or ice cream.

NOTES FROM THE KITCHEN

NOTES FROM THE GARDEN

Chapter Nine

TARRAGON

Tarragon is one of the four herbs used in the classic French blend *fines herbes*. Its three companions—chervil, parsley, and chives—are not nearly bold enough to challenge the flavor of tarragon. They serve alongside the tarragon to enhance its flavor.

There are two main varieties of tarragon, French and Russian, with the Russian exuding little flavor. When purchasing plants for your herb garden, be sure to rub the leaves between your fingers. French tarragon will differentiate itself by the pungent smell it puts off.

Tarragon likes to live outdoors, but wants to live in not-quite-full sun. Since tarragon's root system is shallow, it will faint if not placed in a bit of shade. As with almost all plants, mulch can help protect the roots.

You can also grow tarragon indoors, in a wide pot with about four hours of sun per day. Always allow the soil to completely dry before watering, as tarragon hates wet feet indoors or out.

The following recipes are some great ways to incorporate tarragon into your cooking. Try them and we think you'll agree.

BRAISED PORK LOIN STUFFED WITH CHEESE AND MUSHROOMS

Serves 6–8

3 tablespoons olive oil
1/2 cup shiitake mushrooms, chopped
1/3 cup red onion, chopped
1 garlic clove, minced
1 tablespoon minced parsley
2 tablespoons minced French tarragon
1/2 cup Gorgonzola, mashed until smooth
5 to 6 pounds boneless pork loin
2 cups chicken stock
1 cup chardonnay
Salt and freshly ground pepper, to taste

In 1 tablespoon of the olive oil, sauté the mushrooms and onions. Add the garlic, parsley, and tarragon and sauté briefly. Add salt and pepper. Remove from heat and allow to cool. Stir the mixture into the cheese. With a sharp knife or a metal skewer, pierce each end of the roast. Make a hole about the size of a silver dollar. Continue to work through the roast until the hole is from one end of the roast to the other end. You may have to use your fingers to help with this. Fill a pastry bag with the cheese and herb mixture. Squeeze the filling into the roast until it is firmly packed. Preheat oven to 325°F.

Heat the remaining 2 tablespoons olive oil in an oven-safe pan on top of the stove. Season the roast with salt and pepper and brown on all sides.

Add the wine and the stock. Bring this to a simmer, cover, and transfer to the oven. Bake for 1½ hours or until a meat thermometer inserted in the roast reads 160°F. Remove from the oven and allow the roast to rest about 15 minutes before serving.

Cooking Tip

When making stocks, a good way to store them is in the freezer in ice trays. When the cubes have set up, remove them and put them in a freezer bag. Just remove the amount you need for a future dish.

Don't be afraid to use a good chicken stock from a can when you can't find the time to make it yourself. Just be cautious of the amount of salt used in your dish.

RAISIN AND ALMOND PILAF

Serves 4

2 tablespoons olive oil
2 cloves garlic, minced
1 cup brown rice
Salt and freshly ground black pepper to taste
1 tablespoon fresh tarragon, minced
1 tablespoon unsalted butter
1/2 cup raisins soaked in 1/2 cup white wine
2 cups chicken stock
1/2 cup slivered almonds

Sauté the garlic lightly in the olive oil in a 2-quart saucepan. Add the brown rice, salt and pepper, and tarragon. Cook briefly, stirring, and add the butter and raisins. Cook and stir until the rice has browned lightly, then add chicken stock. Cover the pot tightly and simmer about 20 minutes or until rice is fluffy and tender. During last 5 minutes of cooking, add the almonds.

TARRAGON PESTO

1 cup fresh tarragon leaves or 2 bunches
1 cup fresh flat leaf parsley or about 2 bunches
$^{1}/_{2}$ cup slivered almonds
1 cup Parmesan cheese
2 cloves garlic, peeled
Juice and zest of 1 lemon
$^{1}/_{4}$ cup cold pressed olive oil
$^{1}/_{4}$ teaspoon salt
$^{1}/_{4}$ teaspoon pepper

Place all ingredients in a food processor and pulse a few times until mostly smooth. Be sure to scrape down the sides of processor occasionally. This is a nice twist on basil pesto and can be used in place of basil pesto. Be sure to try this recipe as a spread on toast points and serve at your next party. Your guests will thank you.

BLACKENED TUNA WITH CITRUS TARRAGON VINAIGRETTE

2 pounds fresh tuna steaks cut about 1 inch thick

1 tablespoon cold pressed olive oil

Salt and pepper to taste

Vinaigrette

1 cup fresh orange juice

Zest of 1/2 an orange

1/4 cup lemon juice

Zest of 1 lemon

1 shallot, minced

2 tablespoons Dijon mustard

1/2 cup cold pressed olive oil

1/4 teaspoon salt

1/4 teaspoon pepper

Brush both sides of tuna steaks with olive oil and sprinkle with salt and pepper. Place tuna in a very hot dry sauté pan and cook for 1 to 1 1/2 minutes on each side. Set aside on a platter.

Mix orange juice, orange zest, lemon juice, lemon zest, shallot, and Dijon mustard in a small bowl. Whisk together while you drizzle in olive oil until vinaigrette becomes emulsified. Pour some of the vinaigrette over the warm tuna steaks and serve the remaining vinaigrette in bowl for guests.

BASIC BERNAISE SAUCE

$^{1}/_{4}$ cup white wine vinegar

$^{1}/_{4}$ cup white wine

2 teaspoons minced shallots

3 tablespoons fresh chopped tarragon leaves

Salt and pepper to taste

3 large egg yolks

2 sticks unsalted butter, melted

Add vinegar, white wine, shallots, 1 tablespoon tarragon leaves, salt, and pepper to a sauce pan. Bring to a boil and simmer over medium heat for 5 minutes or until mixture reduces by half.

Pour the cooled mixture into a blender, along with the egg yolks and a pinch of salt, and blend for 30 seconds. With blender running, slowly pour the hot butter through the opening in the lid. Add the remaining tarragon leaves and blend until combined. Keep at room temperature until serving. This is a great sauce for beef or steamed potatoes.

ASPARAGUS WITH TARRAGON BUTTER SAUCE

Serves 4

1 bunch fresh asparagus
2 tablespoons unsalted butter
1 tablespoon freshly minced tarragon
Salt and freshly ground black pepper to taste
Lemon peel for serving

Wash asparagus and break off tender part, discarding woody ends. (Break where asparagus breaks naturally.) In boiling salted water, cook asparagus for 1 minute. Place in a bowl of ice water. This allows the asparagus to retain its natural color.

Melt the butter in a sauté pan. Add tarragon. Place the asparagus spears in the pan; salt and pepper to taste. Sauté the asparagus until tender. Servings of asparagus look especially pretty when tied together in individual-serving-size bundles. Use lemon peel cut in strips to accomplish this.

TARRAGON TASTY ROLLS

Serves 12

2 3/4 cups all-purpose flour, divided
1 package active yeast
1 tablespoon dried parsley
1 tablespoon dried tarragon
1 tablespoon dried oregano flakes
1/2 teaspoon celery seed
2 tablespoons sugar
1/2 teaspoon salt
1 cup warm water
1 egg
2 tablespoons olive oil

Combine 1 1/2 cups flour, yeast, herbs, celery seed, sugar, and salt in a large mixing bowl. Then add the following ingredients: water, egg, and oil. Beat on low speed for 30 seconds, scraping bowl occasionally. Stir in remaining 1 1/4 cups of flour, beating on high speed for 1 minute. Refrain from kneading the dough. Cover and allow dough to rise in a warm place until doubled, usually about 30 minutes. Preheat oven to 375ºF.

Stir dough and spoon into greased muffin cups. Cover and allow dough to rise again in a warm place until doubled, 20 to 30 minutes. Bake for 15 to 18 minutes.

WHITE CHOCOLATE FRUIT TORTE

Serves 8

Torte

$^3/_4$ cup unsalted butter, softened
$^1/_2$ cup confectioners' sugar
$1^1/_2$ cups unbleached all-purpose flour

Filling

1 (10-ounce) package white chocolate, melted
1 (8-ounce) package cream cheese, softened
$^1/_2$ cup heavy cream

Topping

1 (20-ounce) package pineapple chunks, drained, reserving $^1/_2$ cup of juice
1 pint fresh strawberries, washed and sliced in half
1 (11-ounce) can mandarin oranges
2 kiwis, peeled and sliced

Glaze

3 tablespoons sugar
2 teaspoons cornstarch
$^1/_2$ teaspoon fresh lemon juice
Reserved pineapple juice

Preheat oven to 300ºF. In a mixing bowl, cream butter and sugar. Gradually add flour, mixing well. Press this mixture into an ungreased 10-inch springform pan to form the crust. Bake for 25 to 30 minutes, or until lightly browned. Set aside to cool.

Melt chocolate in the microwave or over a double boiler, and place in a large mixing bowl. Add cream cheese and heavy cream. Beat until smooth. Spread over crust. Chill about 30 minutes before making next layer.

Arrange pineapple, sliced strawberries, oranges, and kiwis over cream cheese layer. Set aside again.

In a saucepan over medium heat combine the sugar, cornstarch, lemon juice, and reserved pineapple juice. Bring mixture to the boiling point and boil for 2 minutes or until thickened, stirring constantly. Cool. Brush this over the fruit and chill for at least 1 hour before serving. Store in the refrigerator.

NOTES FROM THE KITCHEN

NOTES FROM THE GARDEN

Chapter Ten

CHIVES

If you want the benefit of onion without the tears, then please plant some chives in your herb garden. The thin, green, tubular stems of the chive plant are available from early spring until late fall. The flowers of the chive are edible too, and they can be used to make an attractively colored herbal vinegar.

For fast growing results, buy a clump of chives from the nursery in the spring, or maybe ask a neighbor for a small clump from their garden, as chives need to be separated every three or four years anyway.

Plant chives in a sunny, well-drained location and allow the stems to reach about 6 inches before snipping them. Be sure to leave at least 2 inches of growth, to allow the stem to continue to bear. For optimum flavor, harvest before the plant blooms.

As an added bonus, chives are successful companion plants to roses in helping to prevent black spot. They may also help to deter Japanese beetles, apple scab, peach leaf-curl, and mildew on cucumbers. They also are in good company with carrots, grapes, and tomatoes.

Once harvested, chop the stems, and either freeze or dry them. Enjoy your chives with vegetables, creamed sauces, and egg, cheese, poultry, fish, or shellfish dishes. Toss the minced stems into salads or use to make flavored butters. Use the flowers as edible garnish in salads, or add to flavored vinegars as mentioned before.

BAKED POTATOES WITH BRIE

Serves 4

4 medium baked Idaho or russet potatoes, hot
2 ounces ripe brie cheese, cut into 1-inch cubes
4 tablespoons (1/2 stick) unsalted butter or margarine, room temperature
1 egg yolk
1 tablespoon minced chives (or finely minced green onion tops) or to taste
1/2 teaspoon salt
1/4 teaspoon freshly ground black pepper
Pinch of ground nutmeg, or to taste

Slice 1/2-inch lengthwise off each baked potato. Taking care not to pierce the skin, scoop out the flesh, leaving a 1/4-inch thick shell. Mash the potato flesh until smooth in a medium-size bowl. Add the brie, butter, egg yolk, chives, salt, pepper, and nutmeg. Mix well. Stuff each potato shell with the mixture, mounding it in the center; transfer to a shallow baking dish. At this point the potatoes can be stored. Refrigerate, tightly covered, for up to 24 hours.

Preheat oven to 375°F. Bake the potatoes, uncovered, until the cheese has melted and the stuffing is heated through, 12 to 15 minutes. Put under the broiler 5 inches from the flame, until lightly browned, 3 to 5 minutes. Serve as a side dish with steak, roasts, poultry, or broiled fish.

CAVIAR EGGS

Serves 6

6 hardboiled eggs
6 tablespoons caviar (red or black)
1 tablespoon chopped chives or green onion
1 tablespoon chopped parsley
1 tablespoon mayonnaise or sour cream
1 teaspoon freshly ground black pepper
Salt to taste
Russian dressing

Shell the eggs, cut them in half, and remove the yolks. Mash the yolks well and combine with remaining ingredients. When yolk mixture is thoroughly whipped together, heap it into the whites with a spoon, or pipe it in, using the rosette end of a pastry tube.

For a first course, serve 2 halves per person, arranged on greens, and pass a Russian dressing. Or double the recipe when served as a salad course with watercress, Russian dressing, and crisp French bread.

HAM WRAPS

Serves 6

8 ounces cream cheese, softened
4 ounces sour cream
1/4 cup minced onion
2 tablespoons minced chives
1 teaspoon garlic powder
Salt and freshly ground black pepper
1 pound sliced ham

Blend first six ingredients together. Spread mix on ham slices and roll up jelly roll fashion.

Chill for 30 minutes, or longer if possible. Cut each roll in thirds for easier serving and secure with individual toothpicks.

CREAMY CHIVE BUTTER

Serves 8

1/2 cup softened sweet butter

2 tablespoons finely chopped chives

Cream the butter and chives with a spoon, fork, or mixer. You could at this point spoon the mixture into a decorative dish and chill; or you could use your favorite molds to make pats and freeze before unmolding. Unmold and serve the pats alongside your favorite crusty breads. Another way to use chive butter is to add some additional seasonings of choice, melt, and pour over your favorite cooked vegetables just before serving.

About Herbal Butters

Herbal butters are excellent for adding zip to cooked vegetables, pasta dishes, and rice or soups. They also add the final touch for melting over grilled chicken or fish. Making herbal butters is quite simple, and they can be tightly wrapped, stored in the freezer, and utilized as needed.

HERB BUTTER

Serves 8

$^1/_2$ cup butter, melted
$^1/_2$ cup minced chives
$^1/_4$ cup finely sliced spring onions
$^1/_4$ cup freshly minced parsley
$1^1/_2$ teaspoons freshly minced thyme
1 tablespoon freshly squeezed lemon juice
Salt and freshly ground black pepper, to taste

Combine all ingredients and drizzle over your favorite prepared vegetable (wonderful over cooked cabbage). This adds a wonderful flavor and will perk up vegetables to satisfy even the hardest-to-please person at your table!

Cooking Tip

A good ratio to remember when making herbal butters is 2 tablespoons of finely chopped herbs, either singly or in combination, to $^1/_2$ cup softened butter. Herbal butters also may be kept in the freezer for several months. The following recipes are some of our creations for using one of our favorites—chive butter.

CHICKEN AND VEGETABLE PAPILLOTE

Serves 4

A papillote is the French term for curled paper. "En papillote" is a culinary technique in which foods such as fish, meats, and poultry are combined with vegetables in heavy parchment paper that is cut in the shape of a heart. The packet is then folded air tight so the flavor and aromas do not escape. Each packet can be served "as is" and unwrapped by your guest to reveal a wonderful surprise.

4 papillotes (or parchment paper)
Creamy Chive Butter (see page 90)
4 boneless, skinless chicken breasts
A medley of fresh or frozen vegetables, mixed together (we suggest carrots, green onions, zucchini or yellow squash, and green bell pepper)
Zest and juice from 1 lemon
1 clove garlic, minced
Olive oil
Salt and freshly ground black pepper to taste

Preheat oven to 350°F. Cut the parchment paper into the shape of a heart and butter heavily with the chive butter. Place one chicken breast along with $^{1}/_{2}$ cup of vegetable medley onto each paper. Add zest and lemon juice, garlic, salt and pepper, and lastly olive oil to papillote. Then seal by folding. Bake on a cookie sheet for 30 to 45 minutes. Cut an X on the top and serve in the parchment paper for a new and exciting dish that is sure to make your family and dinner guests applaud.

CHIVE MUFFINS

Serves 12

2 cups all-purpose flour
1/3 cup minced chives
1/3 cup chopped parsley
1 tablespoon baking powder
1 tablespoon sugar
1 tablespoon brown sugar
1/2 teaspoon salt
1/2 teaspoon pepper
1 egg
1/4 cup butter, melted
1 cup buttermilk

Preheat oven to 400°F. Combine the first eight ingredients in a bowl. In a separate bowl, combine the egg, butter, and the buttermilk. Combine the wet ingredients with the dry, stirring just until moistened. Fill greased muffin cups 2/3 full and bake for 15 to 18 minutes. Cool on a wire rack for 5 minutes before removing muffins from pan.

CHOCOLATE MOUSSE SOUFFLÉ

Serves 8

4 (1-ounce) squares semi-sweet chocolate, broken into pieces
3 eggs, separated
1/8 teaspoon almond extract
3/4 teaspoon cream of tartar
1/2 cup sugar
1 cup chilled heavy cream
Additional grated chocolate for garnish

Heat the chocolate pieces in 2-quart double boiler over very low heat, until melted. Stir the chocolate continuously to prevent burning. Stir in the egg yolks and almond extract. Cook over low heat, stirring frequently for about 4 minutes, or until mixture is smooth and shiny; remove from heat. Beat the egg whites and cream of tartar in large bowl until foamy. Beat in the sugar, 1 tablespoon at a time; continue beating until stiff and glossy to form a meringue. Fold the chocolate mixture into meringue mixture. Beat the heavy cream in chilled bowl until stiff. Fold into the chocolate mixture. Spoon into eight 6-ounce custard cups or glass dishes. Refrigerate at least 2 hours, but no longer than 48 hours. Top with grated chocolate.

NOTES FROM THE KITCHEN

NOTES FROM THE GARDEN

Chapter Eleven

ROSEMARY

You will love growing rosemary in your herbal garden or wherever your herbs may live. Upon bringing your rosemary plants home from the nursery, place them in a sunny location where you want them to stay, since they do not transplant well. Most soils are rich enough to grow rosemary. However, an occasional small dose of fertilizer goes a long way.

Rosemary harmonizes well with any meat, especially in its roasted form. Rosemary is in good company with chives, thyme, chervil, parsley, and bay leaves in recipes. Please use both the flowers and leaves for garnishing and cooking.

Feel free to harvest rosemary throughout the year. Cut 4-inch pieces from the tips of the branches, being careful not to remove more than 20 percent of the growth at a time.

ROSEMARY GRILLED CHICKEN

Serves 4

1 whole chicken (cleaned)
Several sprigs rosemary
Olive oil
Salt and freshly ground black pepper to taste

Thoroughly clean the chicken, and then cut down the middle of the breast, exposing the inside carcass. Rub the chicken (both sides) generously with remaining ingredients. Heat your grill to high heat, then to a low temperature. Lay chicken skin side down; then place a large pan on top of chicken; then lay a large stone on the pan to press the chicken down. Cook in this manner over low heat until the chicken is brown and crisp.

DELIGHT OF THE FOOTHILLS COOLIES

Serves 8–10

1 stick butter (not margarine)
2 cups sugar
1/2 cup milk
1/4 cup cocoa
1/2 cup peanut butter
3 cups quick cooking oats
1/2 cup nuts
1 cup cocoa

Mix the butter, sugar, milk, and cocoa in a saucepan. Bring to a boil and boil for 2 minutes. Add remaining ingredients. Mix well. Drop from a teaspoon on buttered platter or pour into a 9 x 13 x 2-inch pan to set. If the pan is used, cut in 1-inch squares before serving.

ROASTED POTATO SALAD

Serves 6-8

1 1/2 pounds new red potatoes, quartered and cubed
3 tablespoons olive oil
4 teaspoons chopped fresh rosemary
2 cloves garlic, minced
Salt and freshly ground black pepper to taste
1 (6-ounce) can black olives, drained
1 large green bell pepper, cut into small pieces
1 dozen cherry tomatoes, halved
3/4 cup mayonnaise

Preheat oven to 450°F. Place the potatoes in a 13 x 9 x 2-inch pan. Combine the olive oil, rosemary, garlic, salt, and pepper, and drizzle over the potatoes, tossing gently to coat. Roast in oven, uncovered, for 35 to 40 minutes, or until tender. Allow to cool. In large bowl, add the remaining ingredients to the cooled potatoes and toss to mix well. Chill the salad (covered) for several hours before serving. When you serve Roasted Potato Salad, add sprigs of fresh rosemary on the side for a refreshing look that is sure to be appealing not only to the palate but also to the eyes.

CHICKEN SALAD WITH ROSEMARY

Serves 6

3 celery ribs
3 cups cubed, cooked chicken
1/2 cup fat-free mayonnaise
1/2 cup fat-free sour cream
1 tablespoon fresh rosemary, chopped
Salt and freshly ground black pepper to taste

Slice the celery thinly and combine in a bowl with the chicken. Blend together the mayonnaise, sour cream, rosemary, salt, and pepper. Pour the dressing over the chicken and celery, stirring until the ingredients are thoroughly mixed. Serve immediately or refrigerate for up to 24 hours.

SAUTÉED SCALLOPS WITH ROSEMARY AND LEMON

Serves 4

2 tablespoons extra virgin olive oil
1 clove garlic, peeled and sliced
3/4 teaspoon dried rosemary
1 pound of fresh or frozen scallops
Salt and freshly ground pepper to taste
1 tablespoon lemon juice

Put oil and garlic in a frying pan and cook the garlic until golden. Add the rosemary, scallops, salt, and pepper and sauté over high heat until scallops are thoroughly cooked, about 2 to 3 minutes. Do not overcook. Add the lemon juice and turn up the heat for a few seconds. Serve hot.

Rosemary Lore

Our friend rosemary has no doubt caused her share of controversy through the ages. For example, when the rosemary bush grows vigorously in the family's herb garden it means that the woman leads the household. Pruning the rosemary bush probably has fallen into the hands of many a humiliated husband!

It was believed that rosemary possessed powers of protection against evil spirits, or so people of the Middle Ages thought. Men and women of that time would often place sprigs of rosemary under their pillows to ward off demons and prevent bad dreams.

In ancient Greece students believed that twining sprigs of rosemary in their hair would improve their memory, so rosemary garlands were donned while studying for exams.

Rosemary is best known as a symbol of remembrance, friendship, and love.

CORNISH HENS WITH ROSEMARY

Serves 4–6

2 tablespoons olive oil
6 to 8 lemons, juiced (to equal 1 cup)
3 tablespoons rosemary, chopped
4 to 6 Cornish hens, split
1/2 cup breadcrumbs
16 ounces ricotta, drained
4 tablespoons lemon rind
8 cloves garlic, chopped
Salt
Freshly ground pepper
3 cups chicken broth

Mix together the olive oil, lemon juice, and half the rosemary. Place the hens in the marinade, skin side down, as long as possible, preferably overnight.

Preheat oven to 400°F. Remove and drain the Cornish hens, reserving the marinade. Combine the breadcrumbs, ricotta, lemon rind, remaining rosemary, and garlic. Taste and season the mixture with salt and pepper. Loosen the skin of the birds from the breasts, while still leaving it attached, then ease the stuffing under the skin. If the skin tears, it may be sewn up with a trussing needle and string. Place the hens, skin side up, in a baking pan with the marinade, and roast 1 hour. When done, remove from pan. (May be done ahead to this point, and reheated until crisp under broiler.) Degrease the juices. To make the sauce, add the stock to the pan and bring to a boil, stirring the sides and bottom to deglaze the pan. Boil to reduce, tasting occasionally until flavorful, about 20 minutes.

ROSEMARY AND FETA CHEESE DIP

Serves 8

1 cup plain yogurt

1 cup crumbled feta cheese

Leaves from 2 sprigs fresh rosemary, coarsely chopped

1 to 2 cloves of garlic, finely chopped

Salt and freshly ground black pepper

Milk, as needed

Place all ingredients except milk in food processor or blender and blend until smooth. Add a small amount of milk if mixture is too thick to blend. Serve as a dip with fresh vegetables.

ROSEMARY POTATOES

Serves 4

8 small red potatoes, scrubbed and quartered
8 whole cloves garlic, peeled
3 tablespoons olive oil
Salt to taste
1/2 teaspoon freshly ground pepper
1/3 cup minced fresh rosemary
1/2 cup chopped green onions

Preheat oven to 400°F. Place the potatoes and garlic in a single layer in a baking dish. Drizzle with the olive oil and toss potatoes to coat evenly. Sprinkle with the salt, pepper, and rosemary and toss again. Roast for 30 minutes or until potatoes are crisp on the outside and tender inside. Sprinkle with the green onions and serve.

NOTES FROM THE KITCHEN

NOTES FROM THE GARDEN

Chapter Twelve

BAY LEAF

The best way to grow bay seems to be by purchasing a bay tree. The trees enjoy a sunny location, and upon the arrival of cold weather need to be brought indoors to a bright area. If you live in a climate that stays warm even in the winter, you may plant the bay tree in the soil and expect to have a tree up to 50 feet tall! Container plants will reach a height of about 5 to 10 feet.

Bay is valuable for the allspice flavor it brings to soups, stocks, stews, and sauces. I was pleasantly surprised to learn that the flavors of baked custard and vanilla pudding can be greatly enhanced by steeping a bay leaf in the milk before preparing them. You can also toss a bay leaf in the pot when cooking beans, pastas, or rice to add flavor.

When roasting a chicken or turkey, try rubbing the skin and cavity with mustard, then tuck two bay leaves into the cavity for an interesting flavor. Please remember to take the bay leaf out of your dishes before serving.

BAY AT THE MOON CASSOULET

Serves 8

1 pound assorted dry beans (about 2$^1/_2$ cups)
4$^1/_2$ cups cold water
1 tablespoon instant beef bouillon granules
Pinch of ground cloves
4 bay leaves
3 to 3$^1/_2$ pounds chicken, skinned and cut
$^3/_4$ pound boneless pork, cut into bite-sized pieces
$^3/_4$ pound boneless beef, cut into bite-sized pieces
1 to 2 tablespoons olive oil
2 large onions, cut into wedges
2 medium carrots, peeled and sliced
3 cloves garlic, minced
1$^1/_4$ cups white wine (chardonnay)
1 (4$^1/_2$-ounce) can tomatoes, cut up
2 tablespoons dried thyme, crushed
Salt and freshly ground black pepper to taste
$^3/_4$ cup dry breadcrumbs
3 tablespoons butter, melted (not margarine)
2 tablespoons chopped parsley

Combine the beans and enough water to cover in a Dutch oven. Bring to a boil, and simmer for 2 minutes. Remove from heat and cover. Let stand for about an hour. Drain beans and rinse.

In same Dutch oven, combine the drained beans, 4$^1/_2$ cups cold water, bouillon, cloves, and bay leaves. Bring to a boil. Reduce heat and simmer, covered, for 1$^1/_2$ hours. Then discard bay leaves. Brown the chicken, pork, and beef in the olive oil in a large skillet, until done. Remove the meat and cook the remaining vegetables in the drippings. Add the meat and vegetables to the Dutch oven, then deglaze the skillet with the white wine to remove the crumbles off the bottom and add them to the Dutch oven. Add the tomatoes, thyme, and salt and pepper to the Dutch oven. Cover and cook for another hour. Allow to cool completely, then store in refrigerator for 24 hours.

Preheat oven to 375°F. Remove Dutch oven from refrigerator and bake for about 45 minutes. Combine the breadcrumbs, butter, and parsley and sprinkle atop the cassoulet. Bake uncovered for about another 15 minutes, or until cassoulet is bubbling and breadcrumbs are browned. Serve and enjoy.

Bay Leaf Lore

Bay leaf is another one of those herbs with a very noble past. Ancient Greeks and Romans both wore crowns made of woven bay leaves to protect and honor their soldiers, poets, kings, priests, and prophets. The early Greeks would bind an important message with bay leaf to ensure its successful delivery. Could this be where the idea of postage stamps was born?

HAM AND SPLIT PEA SOUP

Serves 4

1 medium onion, chopped
1 clove garlic, minced
3 tablespoons olive oil
5 cups chicken stock
1 1/2 cups split green peas, rinsed
1 cup cooked ham, cubed
1 1/2 teaspoons salt
1/2 teaspoon dried rosemary
1/2 teaspoon dried thyme
1/4 teaspoon white pepper
Salt to taste
3 bay leaves

Sauté the onion and garlic, in a Dutch oven, in the olive oil until tender. Add the remaining ingredients and bring to a boil. Reduce heat, cover, and simmer for 1 1/2 hours, or until peas are tender. Discard bay leaves and serve with hard, crusty bread.

SNOW CREAM

Serves 4

Growing up in the foothills of northwestern North Carolina as children, we enjoyed a simple delight when the snow arrived. It consisted of 3 cups of freshly fallen snow, mixed with 1/2 can sweetened condensed milk, a touch of vanilla extract, and a dash of salt. However, if you live in an area that rarely sees snow fall, we have a nice alternative.

2 cups crushed ice
1/2 can sweetened condensed milk
1 tablespoon vanilla extract
Dash of salt

Whirl blender on slowest speed until all of the ice is crushed fine. Then whirl on the highest speed for about 10 seconds. An air pocket may form at the bottom. If this should occur, turn the blender off and let the trapped air out with a spoon. Add the milk, vanilla, and salt and blend again briefly to mix. Eat immediately.

CITRUS BAY TOMATO SOUP

Serves 4

- 2 pounds fresh tomatoes, cored, cut in half, gently squeezed to remove seeds
- 4 cups chicken stock
- 1 cup freshly squeezed orange juice
- 1 orange, rind removed, thinly sliced
- 1 medium carrot, scraped and thinly sliced
- 1 medium onion, chopped
- $^1/_2$ lemon, rind removed, thinly sliced
- 6 peppercorns
- 1 tablespoon parsley, chopped
- 1 tablespoon thyme, chopped
- 1 bay leaf
- 4 tablespoons unsalted butter
- 4 tablespoons unbleached flour
- 1 teaspoon sugar
- Salt to taste
- $^1/_2$ cup heavy cream

Place the first 11 ingredients in a large stock pot. Bring to a boil, cover and simmer on low about $1^1/_2$ hours. Strain through a sieve into a large bowl. Set aside.

Melt the butter in rinsed stockpot over low heat. Stir in the flour, then add strained soup mixture. Simmer another 10 minutes. Stir in sugar and salt and taste. Right before serving, stir in cream. Garnish with additional orange strips and chopped tomato. Serve soup hot or cold.

ITALIAN BAY CHICKEN

Serves 4

2 (15-ounce) cans tomato sauce
1/2 cup golden raisins
1 medium onion, chopped
1 small green pepper, chopped
4 cloves garlic, minced
2 bay leaves
1 tablespoon olive oil
1 teaspoon ground cumin
1 teaspoon parsley, chopped
1 teaspoon oregano, crushed
1 tablespoon red wine vinegar
1/2 teaspoon salt
1/2 teaspoon freshly ground black pepper
4 boneless, skinless chicken breasts

Preheat oven to 350°F. Combine all ingredients except chicken breasts in a mixing bowl. Wash chicken, pat dry, and place in a 9 x 13-inch baking dish. Spoon sauce over chicken. Cover and bake for 1 1/2 hours. Serve with a salad and hard crusted bread.

BAY-ENHANCED POT ROAST

Serves 8

$^1/_2$ cup unbleached all-purpose flour
1 tablespoon paprika
1 teaspoon freshly ground black pepper
1 (4-pound) beef roast
2 tablespoons olive oil
12 small onions, peeled
6 carrots, sliced in 1-inch pieces
4 celery stalks, sliced in 1-inch pieces
4 tomatoes, peeled, seeded, and chopped
1 cup mushrooms, stems discarded, sliced in quarters
4 cloves garlic, minced
1 teaspoon dried basil
1 teaspoon dried parsley
1 teaspoon dried rosemary
2 bay leaves, crushed
Salt to taste

Preheat oven to 400°F. Combine the flour with the paprika and the pepper. Dredge the roast through flour combination. Heat oil in a Dutch oven and brown roast on all sides. Place in a large baking dish and surround the roast with vegetables. Sprinkle the herbs evenly over vegetables. Bake uncovered for 45 minutes. Cover, reduce heat to 350°F, and bake an additional $2^1/_2$ hours or until done.

PICKLED OYSTERS

Serves 6

3 dozen fresh medium oysters
4 cups water
3 small onions, thinly sliced, separated into rings
2 cayenne peppers, halved and seeded
6 whole black peppercorns
2 bay leaves
1/2 cup white wine vinegar
1/2 teaspoon salt
1/2 teaspoon Tabasco sauce

Shuck the oysters and reserve juice. While shucking oysters, bring 4 cups of water to a boil in a heavy saucepan. Plunge oysters into boiling water and remove pan from heat. Allow to stand for 5 minutes, then drain. Use a clean pint jar to layer the oysters, onions, peppers, peppercorns, and bay leaves. In a separate bowl combine vinegar, salt, and Tabasco sauce. Pour over oysters in jar. Cover tightly and place in the refrigerator for at least 3 days.

PORK CHOPS IN SOUR CREAM

Serves 6

6 pork chops
3 cloves garlic, minced
2 tablespoons olive oil
1 cup sour cream
2 tablespoons vinegar
1 tablespoon Worcestershire sauce
$^1/_2$ teaspoon salt
$^1/_2$ teaspoon freshly ground black pepper
$^1/_2$ teaspoon paprika
3 bay leaves, broken in half
2 tablespoons parsley, chopped

Preheat oven to 350°F. Wash the pork chops and pat dry. Rub the garlic over chops. Heat the olive oil in a skillet, and brown pork chops on both sides. Combine the remaining ingredients except the bay leaves and parsley in a bowl. Place pork chops in a baking dish and pour mixture over. Top each pork chop with $^1/_2$ bay leaf and sprinkle with chopped parsley. Bake 45 minutes. Remove bay leaves before serving.

CRISPY CUCUMBERS

Serves 6–8

2 cups white vinegar
1 cup sugar
1 tablespoon whole cloves
1 tablespoon whole allspice
2 cloves garlic, minced
1 bay leaf
1 cinnamon stick
1 tablespoon whole celery seed
1 tablespoon whole mustard seed
1 tablespoon black peppercorns
1 small piece dried gingerroot
5 large cucumbers, washed, unpared, and sliced
1 large onion, sliced thinly and separated into rings

Combine all ingredients except the cucumbers and onions in a heavy saucepan. Boil rapidly for 15 minutes, remove from heat. Cool, then strain. Place thinly sliced cucumbers and onion in a large bowl or jar. Pour cooled marinade over cucumbers and onions. Cover and refrigerate for at least 3 days. This will keep in the refrigerator for several weeks. Use as a condiment or convenient side salad.

TOMATO ASPIC

Serves 4

1 package unflavored gelatin
1/4 cup cold water
2 cups tomato juice
1 medium onion, sliced
2 cloves garlic, crushed
1 celery stalk, roughly chopped
4 black peppercorns
2 bay leaves
1 teaspoon tarragon vinegar
1/4 teaspoon salt
Leaf lettuce, washed and dried, separated into leaves
Mayonnaise
Paprika

Dissolve the gelatin in water and set aside. Combine the tomato juice with the following seven ingredients in a heavy saucepan. Bring to a boil, cover, reduce heat, and simmer about 10 minutes. Strain tomato juice mixture and add to gelatin. Stir to dissolve. Pour mixture into 4 lightly oiled 1/2-cup molds. Chill aspic until firm.

Unmold cups onto a lettuce-lined serving dish. Garnish each mold with a spoonful of mayonnaise. Sprinkle with some paprika.

VEAL POT ROAST WITH VEGETABLES

Serves 8

1 (4-pound) boneless rolled veal shoulder
3 tablespoons unbleached all-purpose flour
2 teaspoons salt
1 teaspoon black pepper
2 tablespoons unsalted butter
2 tablespoons olive oil
1 large onion, thinly sliced
2 medium carrots, scraped and chopped
2 stalks celery, chopped
4 cloves garlic, minced
3 bay leaves
1 tablespoon thyme, crushed
1 1/2 cups dry white wine
2 cups small mushrooms, cleaned

Preheat oven to 300°F. Wipe veal roast dry. Combine flour, salt, and pepper. Dredge roast with flour combination. Melt butter and add olive oil in a Dutch oven. Brown roast on all sides. Add vegetables, herbs, and wine. Cover, cook slowly for 3 hours or until veal is tender. During last 15 minutes of cooking, add mushrooms. Remove roast and place on a decorative platter. Serve with the vegetables and sauce.

HONEY MUSTARD ESSENCE

3 tablespoons honey
6 tablespoons beer
2 tablespoons cognac
2 tablespoons prepared mustard
Heavy cream, whipped at time of serving

Mix honey, beer, cognac, and mustard. Store in airtight jar for 3 days. When needed, combine one part Honey Mustard Essence to three parts heavy cream. Serve with pâté (see following page).

BAY-INFUSED COUNTRY PÂTÉ WITH ESSENCE

Serves 8

2 pounds chicken livers, trimmed
1 cup cognac
1 cup dry white wine
2 teaspoons freshly ground black pepper
1 teaspoon sage, crushed
1/4 teaspoon cayenne pepper
1 teaspoon thyme, crushed
12 bay leaves
1 teaspoon ground coriander
8 cloves garlic, minced
1 1/2 pounds pork sausage
1 loaf stale French bread
1/2 cup heavy cream
Zest of 2 washed oranges
1 1/2 cups chopped pecans
Salt to taste
1 pound bacon, sliced thin
1 pound baked ham, cubed
1 1/2 cups slivered almonds
Additional bay leaves for garnish

Place the livers, cognac, wine, herbs, and garlic in a bowl. Cover and allow to soak overnight in the refrigerator.

Transfer to a food processor and process until smooth. Transfer to another bowl. Set aside. Sauté sausage until brown in a heavy skillet. Drain and process in food processor until chopped fine but not creamy. Combine with liver mixture. Combine the French bread with heavy cream and process together. Combine with the liver mixture. Stir in the orange zest and the pecans. Season with salt.

Preheat oven to 350°F. Assemble three 9 x 4-inch loaf pans. Arrange bacon slices across sides and bottom of loaf pans. Allow bacon to overhang 2 inches. Gently pack pâté mixture into loaf pans, occasionally adding some of the cubed ham. Fold ends of bacon over top of pâté. Cover each pan with aluminum foil.

Place loaf pans in a large 1-inch-deep baking dish. Add hot water to baking dish halfway up the sides of the loaf pans. Bake for $1^1/_2$ hours. Transfer to cooling rack. Allow to cool about 30 minutes. Place small boards or weights over pâtés and refrigerate overnight. Unmold pates onto decorative platters. Just before serving, coat with almonds by patting on sides and top of pâtés. Serve with Honey Mustard Essence (see page 121).

BLACK BEAN SOUP WITH BAY

Serves 4

2 cups black beans
3 quarts water
6 cups beef stock
2 medium onions, peeled and roughly chopped
1 carrot, scraped and chopped
1 small can chopped green chilies
6 cloves garlic, minced
2 tablespoons sherry
1 bay leaf
1 teaspoon thyme
Salt and freshly ground black pepper to taste
Sour cream, for garnish
Sharp cheddar cheese, shredded, for garnish

Wash beans and place in a heavy saucepan. Cover with water and bring to a boil. Simmer for about 30 minutes. Remove from heat and allow to soak overnight. Drain. Return beans to heavy saucepan and add remaining ingredients. Simmer for several hours or until beans are tender. Remove the bay leaf from soup. Pour soup a little at a time into a blender and liquefy. When smooth, return soup to stove and reheat. Garnish with some sour cream and shredded cheddar cheese.

NOTES FROM THE KITCHEN

NOTES FROM THE GARDEN

Chapter Thirteen

THYME

Thyme could be called the universal herb, since it goes with just about everything and it rounds out the flavor of other herbs in company with it. In ancient times, people often sacrificed animals, particularly lambs, to invoke the approval of their gods. The lambs were often sprinkled with thyme to make them more enticing. This idea may have come from the ancient Egyptians, whose embalmers used thyme to prepare mummies for their journeys.

However, thyme may have been used in combination with lamb to reflect the human fondness of the two combined. Lambs have even been encouraged to graze in fields of wild thyme to make them tastier for eating. Interestingly, gardeners used to think a patch of thyme was a home for local fairies. Just as we today provide birdhouses for our feathered friends, gardeners once set aside a bed of thyme for the fairies.

There are 350 species of thyme from which to choose. Many thymes have no culinary value, so before you purchase a thyme plant, be sure to rub the leaves between your fingers. If the leaves offer no fragrance (peppery with a hint of clove), the thyme is probably not a culinary type.

Find a place in your herb garden that gets at least six hours of sun each day, and dig a hole for each plant that is twice the size of the root ball. After sprinkling a tablespoon of sand into each hole, set in the plant and fill with surrounding soil. Tamp the soil down and water thoroughly. Thyme is best enjoyed in the spring, summer, and fall. However, to enjoy thyme in the winter you must prune hard, about 6 inches, during midsummer.

Be sure to run your fingers through the branches to untangle and to stimulate growth. Thyme is no friend to white flies, so plant thyme around bay and lemon verbena to repel them. Thyme is a friend to bees, so plant thyme around fruit trees and roses that need pollinating. Beekeepers are usually fond of thyme and will often plant it around their hives to attract bees to the area. Thyme-flavored honey is considered "nectar of the gods," so this practice has been used for centuries.

Most cooks prize thyme for its ability to marry flavors in the kitchen. If the stew needs a little something extra, add some thyme. Maybe you are trying to cut back on salt, so add some thyme to give a flat taste some sparkle.

To use thyme in cooking, add 1 tablespoon of fresh leaves to a recipe that serves four. The thyme stems are tough, so use only the leaves. We like to use thyme in our kitchen and have enjoyed these recipes with our friends and family. Try them and see if you feel the same!

THYME-SEASONED LEG OF LAMB

Serves 8

6 slices white bread, crust removed
3 cloves garlic
3 tablespoons chopped fresh parsley
2 teaspoons chopped fresh chives
1 teaspoon dried thyme
1 teaspoon dried rosemary
1/4 cup slivered almonds
1 (6 1/2-pound) leg of lamb, butterflied by your butcher

Preheat oven to 350°F. Put 4 slices of bread in the food processor and process for about 20 seconds or until the bread is crumbly. While the processor is running, drop the garlic through the food chute along with the remaining 2 slices of bread, parsley, and the next four ingredients. Process for about 15 seconds. Set aside. Trim off any excess fat from the lamb, and salt and pepper both sides to taste. Place crumb mixture on both sides of the lamb and roll in reserved breadcrumbs. Place lamb in an oven-tempered pan and sauté on stove top until brown on both sides. Cover and roast for 2 to 2 1/2 hours. Remove from oven and let stand for about 20 minutes to rest. This will allow time to make a little sauce to accompany the lamb.

Make a sauce from the drippings, and in the same roasting pan. Remember, in our kitchen we don't waste anything. All you need to do is put the pan on the stove top and pour about 1/2 cup of dry white wine into the pan. Deglaze the pan, loosening the crumbles from the bottom. Allow to reduce by half, and add either 1 cup of lamb stock or 1 cup of chicken stock. Allow again to reduce by half. Season with salt and pepper to taste, and pour over the lamb for a little added flavor that is sure to bring your family and guests back for more.

THYME FOR ARTICHOKE SALAD

Serves 4

Dressing

1 clove garlic

1/2 teaspoon salt

1/2 teaspoon dried thyme

1/2 teaspoon dried basil

1/2 teaspoon dried tarragon

1 tablespoon prepared mustard

4 to 5 tablespoons red wine vinegar

1/3 cup olive oil

Artichoke Salad

1 (6-ounce) jar marinated artichoke hearts, drained and chopped

6 cups mixed salad greens

1 large tomato, cut into wedges

1/4 cup sliced red onion

1/4 cup black olives

Put the garlic and salt in a salad bowl, mash them together with the tines of a fork until the mixture combines to make a paste. Add the dried herbs and mix again. Then add the mustard and red wine vinegar, mixing thoroughly. Slowly drizzle in the olive oil until emulsified. Add the remaining salad ingredients and toss to mix together.

HARVEST PUMPKIN CHEESECAKE

Makes 1 cake

2 1/2 cups graham cracker crumbs
1/2 cup sugar
1 stick butter, melted
1/4 cup finely chopped pecans
3 (8-ounce) packages cream cheese, room temperature
1 can sweetened condensed milk
1 can pure pumpkin
3 eggs
1/4 cup maple syrup
1 1/2 teaspoons ground cinnamon
1 teaspoon nutmeg

Preheat oven to 300°F. Combine first four ingredients in a large mixing bowl. Pour mixture into a springform pan and mold along the sides and bottom, pressing until firm. Beat the cream cheese in another mixing bowl until silky. Add the condensed milk and pumpkin and continue to mix. Add the eggs one at a time and continue to mix after each addition until the batter is smooth. Fold in the remaining ingredients and mix thoroughly. Pour mixture into springform pan and bake for 1 hour and 10 minutes. Turn off the heat, but allow the cheesecake to remain in the oven for about 15 minutes. Then remove the cake and place it on a wire rack, allowing it to cool for another hour. Place in the refrigerator overnight. Remove sides of springform pan before serving.

POACHED SALMON WITH FRESH THYME

Serves 4

$1^1/4$ pounds boneless, skinless salmon filet cut into 4 pieces of equal size
6 sprigs fresh thyme
Salt and freshly ground black pepper to taste

Place salmon in a shallow pan and cover with water. Add thyme, salt, and pepper. Bring to a boil and cover, lower heat and let simmer for 5 minutes. Do not overcook. Serve immediately.

Cooking Tip

After handling, to remove the smells of fish, onions, and garlic from your hands, just wash your hands in a little soap and water, then grab your faucet and rub or twist your hands around the neck of the faucet. The stainless steel will remove any trace of the scent!

ALMOND CRUSTED CHICKEN WITH THYME

Serves 4

4 boneless, skinless chicken breasts
Salt and freshly ground black pepper to taste
2 cups toasted slivered almonds
1 cup all-purpose flour
2 large eggs, lightly beaten
$^{2}/_{3}$ cup mild honey
2 tablespoons fresh thyme, or 1 teaspoon dried
3 tablespoons red wine vinegar
$^{2}/_{3}$ cup plus 2 tablespoons chicken stock, divided
1 teaspoon cornstarch

Preheat oven to 350°F. Cut the chicken in $1^{1}/_{2}$-inch-wide strips or "fingers." Season with salt and pepper. Place the toasted almonds in the bowl of a food processor and process until finely ground but not powdery, about 10 seconds. Empty into a baking dish for dipping. Place the flour in a separate dish and put the beaten eggs in a bowl next to these 2 dishes. Line a large cookie sheet with foil and lightly oil the foil. Dip chicken first in flour and shake off any excess. Then dip in egg to coat. Roll strips in ground almonds until well coated. Place on foil-lined sheet and bake, turning once, for 20 to 25 minutes, or until lightly browned.

Meanwhile, prepare the sauce. Combine honey and thyme in a medium saucepan. Bring to a boil over high heat, then reduce to medium-high.

Cook until slightly caramelized, about 2 minutes. Stir in vinegar and $^2/_3$ cup stock. Simmer, stirring often, for 5 minutes.

In a small bowl or cup, whisk together the cornstarch and remaining 2 tablespoons stock. Add to the sauce and continue simmering, stirring constantly, until shiny and slightly thickened, 3 to 4 minutes. When the chicken is done, transfer to a warmed serving platter. Drizzle a small amount of the sauce over the top and serve the rest on the side.

PECAN RICE

Serves 4

$^{3}/_{4}$ pound fresh mushrooms, sliced
$^{1}/_{2}$ cup minced shallots
$^{2}/_{3}$ cup butter
$1^{1}/_{3}$ cups uncooked brown rice
1 teaspoon dried thyme
Salt and pepper to taste
1 cup chopped pecans, toasted
4 cups chicken broth
Whole pecans, toasted
Parsley

Preheat oven to 375°F. In a Dutch oven, sauté the mushrooms and shallots in butter 5 to 7 minutes, or until golden. Stir in the rice and cook, stirring with a wooden spoon, approximately 3 minutes or until rice is hot. Season with the thyme, salt, and pepper. Stir in the chopped pecans and chicken broth. Heat to boiling. Remove from heat. Cover and bake approximately $1^{1}/_{2}$ hours, or until liquid is absorbed and rice is tender. Garnish with the whole pecans and chopped parsley.

OVEN-DRIED TOMATOES WITH THYME

Serves 4

8 medium plum tomatoes
1 teaspoon salt
1 teaspoon sugar
2 teaspoons thyme
Olive oil

Preheat oven to 250°F. Remove the stem ends from tomatoes. Cut in half lengthwise. Arrange cut-side-up on an open rack set on a sheet pan. Combine salt, sugar, and thyme. Sprinkle over tomatoes. Drizzle olive oil over tomatoes. Place rack in the oven. Bake for 4 hours. Serve as a garnish for poultry, veal, lamb, or fish.

TIM AND JAN'S THYME AND THYME AGAIN

Serves 8–10

8 ounces cream cheese, softened
4 ounces sour cream
2 tablespoons chopped thyme leaves
1 tablespoon coarsely chopped basil
1 tablespoon chopped parsley
Salt and freshly ground black pepper, to taste
Additional herbs for garnish

Blend all ingredients thoroughly and chill overnight. Place in serving bowl and garnish with basil, parsley, and thyme leaves. Serve on a tray of crackers and/or vegetable sticks. Guests will visit this appetizer "thyme and thyme again."

PITA PIZZA THYME

Serves 6

1 package flat pita bread (about 12 flats)
4 tablespoons olive oil
4 tablespoons dried thyme, crushed
1 tablespoon dried oregano, crushed

Cut each flat into 6 triangles. Brush the top of each triangle with olive oil. Sprinkle lightly with the thyme and oregano. Toast in hot oven until golden brown. Serve hot as an appetizer or use for dinner bread.

LEMON THYME LIFT

Serves 2

2 cups water
1/2 teaspoon fresh lemon thyme leaves
1/2 teaspoon honey

Bring water to a boil and remove from heat. Add lemon thyme leaves and steep for 5 minutes. Strain into cups and add honey. Relax and enjoy.

SUN-DRIED TOMATO THYME MUFFINS

Makes 12

Vegetable shortening spray
1/3 cup sun-dried tomatoes, chopped fine
2 cups flour
1 tablespoon baking powder
1/2 teaspoon salt
1/4 teaspoon freshly ground black pepper
1 cup milk
1 egg
1/4 cup olive oil
1/2 cup grated Parmesan cheese
2 teaspoons fresh thyme, chopped

Preheat oven to 375°F. Spray (2 1/2-inch) muffin cups with vegetable shortening spray. If sun-dried tomatoes are packed in oil, remove from oil, rinse under running water, and pat dry. Chop fine and set aside. In a large bowl, combine the flour, baking powder, salt, and pepper. Set aside. In a second bowl, whisk together the milk, egg, and oil until smooth. Add the cheese, tomatoes, and thyme, and blend thoroughly. Add dry ingredients to wet ingredients and stir until blended. Spoon into muffin cups, filling 2/3 full. Bake for about 20 minutes, or until tester comes out clean. Serve warm.

NOTES FROM THE KITCHEN

NOTES FROM THE GARDEN

Chapter Fourteen

SAGE

According to folklore and history, the herb sage stands for wisdom, health, and age. How often we have heard the wise men of old called sages! We wonder if they liked the herb as well as we do. With its pebbly, grayish-green, suede-like leaves and its beautiful, edible lavender flowers, along with an aroma of citrus mixed with camphor, sage is the must-have herb for every herb garden.

There are numerous types of sage, but by far the easiest to grow is the green sage. Take note that the cousins of green sage—purple, gold, or tricolored—are sensitive to severe winters.

Another thing to remember when growing sage is to trim back the plant into a mound shape in the fall. Some experts advise trimming in the spring, but if you do, you will miss the beautiful burst of purple spikes that rise from the sage plant in the spring.

Besides, trimming in the fall makes the plant clean and tidy for winter. As the winter passes, check on the sage and trim away any dead sprigs as they appear. You can harvest the leaves through the fall and early winter. After that the taste becomes almost unpleasant.

Sage is a nice companion plant for rosemary. When the two are planted close by, sage will help keep rosemary from developing powdery mildew.

The mustard-cabbage family especially enjoys having sage nearby, as it will keep cabbage moths away. Isn't it nice to have such good friends in the herb garden!

Once again, I find it easier to go to the nursery in the spring to buy my sage plants. And, as always, I prefer organically grown plants, as we hope you will too. Your plants will appreciate having at least six hours of full sun each day. Bury your plants in healthy soil and water thoroughly. Check on them often to make sure they are getting enough water, and water established plants once a week during dry periods.

Gather the leaves as needed or preserve them for future use. To dry sage, spread on cloth or paper in an area that will stay dry, such as your attic. When thoroughly dry, store in an airtight container. You'll find that dried sage has a stronger and slightly different flavor than the fresh.

Don't forget to make use of sage flowers. The flowers make a nice addition in salads, fruit desserts, or in hot apple cider. The leaves are good in a large variety of dishes such as stuffings, cheese, pork, poultry, vegetables, butters, jellies, and vinegars.

PIGGY PIE

Makes 1 pie

- 1 double crust for a 9-inch pie (use store bought or follow your favorite recipe)
- 1½ pounds ground pork
- 3 cloves garlic, minced
- 1 medium onion, chopped
- 1 cup chopped celery
- 2 medium potatoes, peeled and shredded
- 1½ cups water
- 1 tablespoon dried sage
- 1 teaspoon dried thyme
- ½ teaspoon dried savory
- ¼ teaspoon ground allspice
- ¼ teaspoon ground cinnamon
- 1 bay leaf
- Salt and freshly ground black pepper, to taste
- 1 tablespoon all-purpose flour
- 2 tablespoons cold water

Glaze

- 1 egg (slightly beaten)
- 1 teaspoon water

Line a 9-inch pie plate with bottom half of pastry, trimming the edge even. Set aside. Cook the ground pork in a large skillet. Drain. Return the pork to the skillet and sauté with the garlic, onion, and celery. Add the potatoes, 1½ cups water, and seasonings, allowing mixture to come to a boil. Reduce heat, cover, and simmer for 15 minutes. In separate bowl, combine the 2 tablespoons of water with flour, stirring until smooth. Stir into pork mixture and bring to a boil again. Reduce heat, cover, and simmer for another 5 minutes. Mixture should be thickened. At this point, remove the bay leaf.

Preheat oven to 400°F.

Combine egg and water to brush over bottom pastry in pie plate. Bake for 5 minutes. Remove pie plate from oven and pour pork mixture into bottom crust. Place remaining pastry over top, cutting slits in top for steam to escape. Trim and seal the edges. Brush remaining egg glaze over top crust and return to oven. Bake 10 minutes and then reduce heat to 350°F. Bake 15 minutes longer or until golden brown. This pie can be a whole meal in itself by adding a nice salad and dessert.

TIM AND JAN'S BREAKFAST CASSEROLE

Serves 6

1 pound breakfast sausage, cooked and drained
6 eggs
Salt and freshly ground black pepper to taste
1 teaspoon dried mustard
4 ounces sharp cheddar cheese, shredded
Sour cream
1 tablespoon dried sage

Preheat oven to 350°F. Crumble sausage in a 9-inch casserole dish. Mix the eggs, salt, and pepper with dry mustard in a bowl until well blended. Pour over the sausage and sprinkle with half the cheese. Spread the sour cream and the tablespoon of sage over casserole. Top with remaining cheese. Bake for 30 minutes. Cut into wedges and serve warm.

ALL-IN-ONE BREAKFAST CASSEROLE

Serves 4

6 breakfast sausage links
2 cups mild cheddar cheese, shredded
1 tablespoon all-purpose flour
1 cup Monterey Jack cheese, shredded
1 tablespoon dried sage
6 large eggs, lightly beaten
$^1/_2$ cup half-and-half
1 teaspoon Worcestershire sauce
Salt and freshly ground black pepper to taste

Sauté sausage in a skillet until browned. Drain on paper towels and set aside. Combine cheddar cheese and flour. Sprinkle evenly on bottom of greased $1^1/_2$-quart shallow, round baking dish. Sprinkle with Monterey Jack cheese and sage; set dish aside. Combine eggs, half-and-half, Worcestershire sauce, salt, and pepper; pour over cheese mixture. Arrange breakfast links over top. Cover and chill 8 hours.

Preheat oven to 350°F. Remove baking dish from refrigerator and allow to come to room temperature (about 30 minutes). Bake uncovered for about 45 minutes. Let stand 5 minutes before serving.

BREAKFAST SKILLET

Serves 4

3 tablespoons olive oil
1 teaspoon minced garlic
1 teaspoon dried sage
1/2 cup cubed potatoes
1/2 cup cubed ham
6 sausage links

Heat the olive oil in a heavy iron skillet. Add the garlic, sage, and potatoes, tossing to coat with olive oil. Add cubed ham and sausage links, sautéing until brown. Serve beside a soft omelet along with your favorite breakfast bread.

Cooking with Eggs

We love to cook eggs, so we want to share some egg tips with you. When you are scrambling eggs, be sure to cook them slowly. Their texture will be much creamier if you take your time and keep moving them around in the pan. When making omelettes, try putting the filling on the side. This makes the eggs more edible.

SQUASH CASSEROLE

Serves 6

2 pounds yellow squash, cubed
1/4 cup unsalted butter
1 cup chopped onion
1 cup chopped celery
3 cloves garlic, minced
1 carrot, shredded
1/2 cup sour cream
1 can cream of chicken soup
1/2 cup seasoned breadcrumbs
1 cup sharp cheddar cheese, shredded
2 eggs, beaten
1 teaspoon salt
1/2 teaspoon freshly ground black pepper
2 tablespoons dried sage, crumbled
1 tablespoon dried thyme, crushed
1 tablespoon dried parsley, crumbled
Cooking spray

Place the squash in a medium saucepan and cover with water. Bring to a boil, reduce heat, and simmer for 10 minutes. Drain and mash squash with a potato masher. Drain again and set aside.

Preheat oven to 350°F. Melt the butter in a large skillet and sauté the onion, celery, and garlic until tender. Remove from heat and add carrot and mashed squash. Stir in remaining ingredients. Spray a casserole dish with cooking spray and place mixture in dish. Sprinkle additional breadcrumbs over top of casserole. Bake for 30 minutes.

FRUIT AND PECAN STUFFING

Serves 6–8

- 1/2 cup orange liqueur
- 1 (6-ounce) package mixed dried fruit bits
- 1/2 cup unsalted butter
- 1 cup chopped onion
- 1 cup chopped celery
- 3 cloves garlic, minced
- 2 tablespoons parsley, chopped
- 1 tablespoon sage, crumbled
- 1 teaspoon thyme, crushed
- 1/2 teaspoon oregano, crushed
- 1 teaspoon salt
- 1/2 teaspoon freshly ground black pepper
- 10 cups dry breadcrumbs
- 2/3 cup broken pecan pieces
- 2 cups chicken stock
- Cooking spray

Bring the orange liqueur to a boil in a small saucepan. Add the dried fruit, and remove from heat. Cover and allow to stand for 15 minutes. Melt the butter in a medium saucepan and sauté the onion, celery, and garlic until tender. Remove from heat and stir in the herbs, salt, and pepper.

Preheat oven to 360°F. Place the dry breadcrumbs in a large bowl and add the fruit mixture (undrained), the vegetable mixture, and the pecans. Drizzle chicken stock over mixture. Spray a 9 x 13-inch baking dish with cooking spray. Gently pack mixture into baking dish and bake for 30 minutes.

WHITE BEAN SOUP

Serves 4

2 cups dry white beans
6 cups water
1/4 cup unsalted butter
1 cup chopped onion
1 cup chopped celery
4 cloves garlic, minced
3 cups cooked chicken, shredded
2 tablespoons fresh parsley, chopped
4 tablespoons dried sage, crumbled
1 tablespoon dried thyme, crushed
Salt and freshly ground black pepper to taste
4 cups chicken stock

Wash and pick over beans. Place in large stockpot and cover with water. Bring to a boil; reduce heat, cover, and cook for 20 minutes. Remove from heat and allow to sit for several hours, or overnight. Melt the butter in a skillet and sauté the onion, celery, and garlic until tender. Add chicken and herbs. Drain beans, return to pot, and add chicken stock. Add vegetables, chicken, salt, and pepper. Cook gently, stirring often, until beans are soft. Serve with hard crusted bread.

CREAMED SHRIMP

Serves 4

2 cups medium shrimp (cleaned and deveined)
1 hardboiled egg
1 cup sliced fresh mushrooms
1/4 cup plus 1 tablespoon unsalted butter
1/2 medium green pepper, chopped
1/2 medium red pepper, chopped
1/2 cup chopped onion
1/4 cup unbleached all-purpose flour
2 cups milk
1 cup vegetable stock
1 teaspoon salt
2 tablespoons dried sage, crumbled
2 tablespoons fresh parsley, minced
Rice or hot cooked noodles

Combine shrimp, egg, and mushrooms in a medium bowl. Set aside. Melt 1 tablespoon butter in saucepan and sauté peppers and onion until tender. Set aside. In a double boiler, melt remaining 1/4 cup butter over boiling water. Add flour and stir constantly. Gradually add milk and vegetable stock, blending well. Cook until mixture has thickened. Remove from heat; stir in salt, sage, and parsley. In a separate bowl combine shrimp mixture, sautéed vegetables, and creamed mixture, stirring well. Serve over rice or noodles.

HERBED SAUSAGE

Serves 8

1 pound ground pork
½ pound ground veal
1 small onion, finely minced
2 cloves garlic, finely minced
¼ cup fresh parsley, chopped
2 teaspoons fresh thyme, chopped
2 teaspoons fresh sage, chopped
1 teaspoon salt
½ teaspoon freshly ground black pepper
Cooking spray

Combine all ingredients in a large bowl and mix well. Form mixture into 18 balls. Flatten the balls into ½-inch-thick patties. Spray a large skillet with cooking spray and cook the patties over medium heat, 4 to 5 minutes on each side. Check to make sure patties are no longer pink inside. Drain on paper towels before serving with pancakes or eggs.

SAGE ROASTED VEGETABLES

Serves 4

1/3 cup unsalted butter

1 tablespoon parsley, chopped

1 tablespoon sage, chopped

3 cloves garlic, finely minced

Salt and freshly ground black pepper, to taste

1/2 pound Brussels sprouts, cut into halves

1/2 pound parsnips, peeled and cubed

1/4 pound baby carrots, scraped

1 sweet potato, peeled and cubed

1 small butternut squash, peeled, seeded, and cubed

Preheat the oven to 375°F. Melt the butter in small saucepan; stir in the parsley, sage, garlic, salt, and pepper. Place the vegetables in a 9 x 13-inch baking dish. Pour on the butter and herb mixture, stirring to coat well. Cover and bake for 30 minutes or until just tender. Stir occasionally while cooking and serve vegetables crisp-tender.

CHICKEN PIE FOR THE NEW SOUTH

Serves 4

- 2 whole (double) chicken breasts on the bone, skin removed
- 4 tablespoons dried sage, crushed
- 2 tablespoons dried thyme, crushed
- 1/2 teaspoon freshly ground black pepper
- 1 1/2 teaspoons salt
- 1 can cream of mushroom soup
- 2 cups chicken stock, reserved from poaching chicken
- 1 cup buttermilk
- 1 cup unbleached all-purpose flour
- 1/2 teaspoon baking soda
- 1 teaspoon baking powder
- 4 tablespoons unsalted butter, melted

Place chicken in a heavy saucepan and cover with water. Bring to boil, cover, and simmer for 30 minutes. Cool and set aside. Reserve chicken stock. When chicken has cooled, remove meat from bones, shred, and place in a 9 x 13-inch baking dish. Sprinkle the sage, thyme, pepper, and 1 teaspoon salt over chicken and mix thoroughly.

Preheat oven to 375°F. Combine reserved chicken stock and soup in a mixing bowl and blend well. Pour over the chicken. Combine the flour, baking soda, baking powder and remaining salt in the same bowl. Add buttermilk and mix thoroughly. Place spoonfuls of the flour mixture over the chicken. Drizzle melted butter over top of flour mixture. Bake for 30 minutes, until crust is golden brown.

PORK ROAST WITH MUSHROOM SAUCE

Serves 8

2 teaspoons fresh rosemary, crushed
1 tablespoon dried sage, crushed
1 teaspoon dried thyme, crushed
1 teaspoon dried parsley, crushed
1 teaspoon ground coriander seed
4 cloves garlic, minced
1 teaspoon kosher salt
1 teaspoon freshly ground black pepper
1 (4-pound) pork loin roast, rolled and tied

Preheat the oven to 425°F. In a small bowl combine the herbs, garlic, salt, and pepper. Coat the roast with the herbs, patting the herbs to make them adhere. Place coated roast on a rack in shallow baking pan. Insert meat thermometer. Roast for 30 minutes. Reduce oven temperature to 350°F. Continue to roast until temperature in center registers 165°F. Plan on 25 minutes per pound. When roasting is completed, remove baking pan from oven and allow the pork to rest, covered loosely with aluminum foil, while preparing Mushroom Sauce (see following page).

MUSHROOM SAUCE

Serves 4

2 tablespoons olive oil
4 cloves garlic, minced
1 small onion, chopped
1 pound mushrooms of your choice, chopped into small pieces
1/2 teaspoon black pepper
1/2 teaspoon salt
1 teaspoon dried thyme, crushed
1 cup sherry
1 cup chicken stock
2 tablespoons soy sauce
2 teaspoons cornstarch
1 tablespoon water

Heat the olive oil in a medium skillet. Sauté the garlic, onion, and mushrooms for 4 to 5 minutes until tender. Add herbs and stir. Pour sherry into pan and simmer until most of the sherry has evaporated. Add the chicken stock and soy sauce. While this is coming to a boil, dissolve the cornstarch in water, then stir into skillet mixture. Simmer another 3 to 4 minutes. Slice pork roast and serve with mushroom sauce.

STUFFED ONIONS

Serves 6

6 large Vidalia onions
1/2 cup unsalted butter
2 cloves garlic, minced
1 cup black olives, chopped
1 cup breadcrumbs
1 cup sharp cheddar cheese, shredded
1 small tomato, chopped
2 tablespoons fresh parsley, chopped
1 tablespoon dried sage
1 teaspoon poultry seasoning
1/2 teaspoon salt
1/4 teaspoon freshly ground black pepper
1/4 teaspoon paprika
Cooking spray

Remove a 1/4-inch slice from top and bottom of each onion. Place the onions in a Dutch oven, cover with water, and bring to a boil. Reduce the heat, cover, and simmer for 20 minutes or until tender. Drain, set aside and cool. Chop the remaining onion slices. Melt butter in skillet and sauté chopped onions and garlic until tender. Remove from heat. Add remaining ingredients except for the paprika and stir to combine.

Preheat oven to 350°F. Scoop the center portion out of each onion. Discard. Fill each onion with the mixture. Sprinkle the tops with paprika. Lightly spray a 9 x 13-inch baking dish. Place onions in baking dish and cover. Bake for 20 minutes. Uncover and bake for an additional 5 minutes.

CHOCOLATE-CHERRY DELIGHT

Serves 6

1/2 cup milk
1 teaspoon vanilla extract
1 teaspoon almond extract
2 (7-ounce) jars marshmallow cream
4 plain milk or dark chocolate candy bars, chopped
1/2 cup almonds
1/2 cup maraschino cherries
2 cups heavy cream (whipped)

Cook the milk, vanilla, almond extract, and marshmallow cream over low heat, stirring until smooth. Cool. Stir in chopped candy bars, almonds, and cherries. Fold in whipped cream. Transfer to an ungreased 9 x 5 x 3-inch loaf pan. Cover and freeze for at least 4 hours. Ten minutes before serving, remove from freezer to unmold and slice. Yummy!

NOTES FROM THE KITCHEN

NOTES FROM THE GARDEN

Chapter Fifteen

PARSLEY

For gardeners who enjoy cooking, both curly and Italian parsley are musts for the herb garden. Not only do humans enjoy parsley, but the swallowtail butterfly caterpillar adores it as a food source as well. Be sure to grow enough parsley for yourself and these soon to be beautiful butterflies.

Parsley prefers full sun to light shade. A humus-rich, well-drained soil will keep its feet happy. If you allow your parsley to go to seed, it will reseed itself.

We prefer to buy our parsley plants from an organic nursery in the spring. Space them 8 to 12 inches apart. You may want to plant the curly parsley as a border in your herb, flower, or vegetable garden. We have seen curly parsley interspersed with a planting of marigolds, and it looked very pleasant to the eye! Six plants should be enough for the average family (and a few swallowtail caterpillars).

Remember to weed the parsley plants often to keep them productive. Also it is a good idea to cut back the outer stems often, and remove all the flower stalks, to keep plants from going to seed.

Parsley leaves can be used in most any dish except dessert. With its mild flavor, you can use parsley as you would fresh spinach—washed and chopped in salads, omelettes, soups, timbales, and stir-fries. The best tasting parsley is the flat-leafed type. The curly-leafed probably is best used to garnish a finished product.

When gathering parsley, cut off the stems at the base on the outside of the plant. The stems tend to be bitter, so be sure to discard them. Parsley leaves can be dried or frozen for future use. When using fresh parsley, keep it wrapped in a damp paper towel in a plastic bag in the refrigerator until you are ready to cook with it.

We love to use parsley in a number of recipes. Here are some of our favorites. Give them a try in your kitchen.

POACHED SALMON

Serves 4

$1\frac{1}{2}$ cups dry white wine
1 shallot, minced
1 bunch parsley
Salt to taste
4 salmon filets

Combine all ingredients except salmon in a non-reactive pan over low heat. Do not allow mixture to boil. Poach the salmon filets in the slightly simmering liquid. Cover pan with parchment paper, not a lid. Allow steam to escape and keep watch over the salmon as it poaches. Poach salmon until just done. Do not overcook—as with any fish, it loses its appeal if overcooked.

PARSLEY-BUTTERED ASPARAGUS

Serves 4

1 bunch asparagus
Ice water
1 tablespoon butter
1/4 cup fresh parsley, chopped
1 clove garlic
Salt and freshly ground black pepper to taste

Wash asparagus. Do not trim by cutting. Trim by snapping stems, allowing asparagus to break at its natural point. Discard tough ends of stems. Blanch asparagus in boiling water for about 30 seconds. Remove and immediately place in ice water to halt cooking process and retain color. Remove the asparagus from the ice water after several minutes and pat dry with paper towels. Cook the butter, parsley, and garlic in a saucepan. Add the asparagus, salt, and pepper, and cook until tender. Serve immediately.

MASHED POTATOES WITH PARSLEY

Serves 6

2 pounds white potatoes
1/2 cup sour cream
1/4 cup milk
1/2 stick butter, softened
Salt to taste
2 tablespoons fresh parsley, chopped
1/4 stick of melted butter
1 teaspoon paprika

Peel the potatoes, chop into small pieces, and cook in boiling, salted water until tender. Drain and mash with a potato masher or beater.

Preheat oven to 250°F. Beat in the sour cream, milk, softened butter, salt, and parsley. Put in a baking dish, and drizzle melted butter and paprika over the top. Bake for 15 minutes or until heated through.

PARSLEY POTATO POCKETS

Serves 4

2 cups potatoes, cubed
$^1/_2$ cup parsley, chopped
4 tablespoons butter
Salt and freshly ground black pepper to taste

Preheat oven to 350°F. Divide potatoes, parsley, and butter onto four large squares of aluminum foil. Sprinkle with salt and pepper. Fold over and seal all sides of foil. Place on cookie sheet and bake for 45 minutes. Open pockets and serve hot. This also works nicely on the grill. You could also add other favorite vegetables to the pockets, cooking them right along with the potatoes.

VENISON-BEEF STEW WITH PARSLEY

Serves 6

2 pounds beef stew meat, cubed
2 pounds venison ham, cubed
2 tablespoons olive oil
Salt and freshly ground black pepper to taste
2 onions, chopped
4 ribs celery, diced
1 green bell pepper, diced
1 (12-ounce) can whole tomatoes
2 (8-ounce) cans tomato sauce
2 bay leaves
1 pound carrots, peeled and diced
2 ears corn
4 to 5 potatoes, peeled and diced
1/2 cup fresh flat-leaf parsley, chopped

Brown beef and venison together in olive oil; then add salt and pepper. Add onions, celery, bell pepper, tomatoes, tomato sauce, and bay leaves to meat mixture. Add hot water to cover and simmer for 20 minutes. Parboil carrots and remove corn from the cob. Add carrots, corn, and potatoes to the stew. Simmer an additional 25 minutes. Add fresh parsley and simmer another 5 minutes. Serve and enjoy.

SHRIMP WITH FETA CHEESE

Serves 4

1 large onion, chopped
1/2 cup olive oil
1 (16-ounce) can tomatoes, drained and chopped
4 tablespoons chopped, fresh flat-leaf parsley
1 teaspoon salt
2 small dried red chiles or 1/2 teaspoon cayenne pepper
2 cloves garlic, minced
2 pounds shrimp, peeled and deveined
1/2 pound feta cheese
1/4 cup vodka, optional

Sauté onion in oil until transparent. Add tomatoes, parsley, salt, chiles, and garlic. Cover and simmer for about 40 minutes.

Preheat oven to 350°F. Add shrimp and feta cheese to the sauce and pour into individual scallop shells or a 3-quart baking dish and bake for 10 to 15 minutes. Remove from oven and, if desired, pour heated vodka over shrimp and flame. You can serve this impressive feast with rice or little boiled new potatoes.

BEER BOIL

Serves 4

2 quarts water

2 quarts beer (5 12-ounce cans)

5 tablespoons salt

2 tablespoons freshly cracked black pepper

2 tablespoons dry mustard

2 tablespoons celery seed

2 cups tarragon vinegar

1/2 cup fresh flat-leaf parsley, unchopped

3 pounds unpeeled shrimp

Combine all the ingredients except for the shrimp. Bring the mixture to a boil. Add the shrimp and boil 8 to 10 minutes. Drain and leave shrimp in shells for about 30 minutes. Serve and enjoy.

TIM AND JAN'S SPICY CAROLINA SHRIMP

Serves 4

1 pound butter
1 (16-ounce) bottle Italian dressing
Juice of 4 lemons
2 ounces of freshly cracked black pepper
4 pounds large shrimp, unpeeled
1/2 cup fresh flat-leaf parsley, chopped

Melt the butter and mix with dressing, lemon juice, and pepper. Pour sauce over shrimp and marinate several hours.

Preheat oven to 325°. Place shrimp in baking dish and cook for about 40 minutes. Sprinkle fresh parsley over shrimp. Serve and enjoy.

RUM SHRIMP

Serves 4

3 dozen large shrimp, peeled except for tails, and deveined
1/2 cup butter
1/2 cup light rum
2 large cloves garlic, minced
Salt and freshly ground black pepper, to taste
1/2 cup fresh flat-leaf parsley, chopped

Place shrimp flat in bottom of shallow baking pan. Melt butter and add rum, garlic, salt, and pepper. Pour mixture over shrimp, distributing garlic evenly. Cover and allow to marinate for 30 to 60 minutes at room temperature.

Preheat broiler. Remove cover from baking pan and place under broiler. Broil shrimp 3 minutes. Turn each shrimp over and broil an additional 3 minutes. Sprinkle fresh parsley over shrimp. This rum-flavored dish is one that can be served in bowls with French bread to soak up liquid, or over cooked rice. Whatever way you decide to serve this dish, you will be a big hit with your friends.

CARROT ZUCCHINI TOMATO BAKE

Serves 4

3 cups sliced carrots
3 small zucchini, sliced
12 cherry tomatoes, peeled
1½ cups milk
2 tablespoons cornstarch
1 cup shredded cheddar cheese, divided
2 tablespoons butter
1 teaspoon salt
Dash cayenne pepper
½ cup slivered almonds
4 tablespoons chopped fresh parsley

Preheat oven to 375°F. Cook carrots in boiling salted water for about 5 minutes. Layer zucchini, carrots, and tomatoes in a 12 x 8 x 2-inch baking dish. In a saucepan, stir cornstarch into the milk. Add ½ cup cheese, butter, salt, and cayenne. Cook until smooth and thickened. Pour over vegetables. Sprinkle with remaining cheese and almonds and parsley. Bake for 30 minutes. Serve and enjoy.

RASPBERRY CARROTS

Serves 4

4 to 5 carrots, thinly sliced

$^{1}/_{2}$ cup water

$^{1}/_{4}$ cup butter

Pinch salt

2 to 4 teaspoons raspberry vinegar

2 teaspoons brown sugar

Fresh parsley, chopped, for garnish

Simmer carrots in a large, covered saucepan with the water, butter, and salt until tender. Add the raspberry vinegar and sugar. Cook, uncovered, another 1 to 2 minutes. Garnish with chopped parsley.

MAMMA'S OKRA AND TOMATOES

Serves 6

1 pound okra

1 tablespoon bacon drippings

1 large onion, chopped

2 large tomatoes, peeled, cored, and chopped

3 tablespoons fresh parsley

1 teaspoon salt

$^{1}/_{4}$ teaspoon freshly cracked black pepper

2 dashes cayenne pepper

$^{1}/_{2}$ teaspoon sugar

Rinse okra and dry well. Remove tops and slice pods crosswise in $^{1}/_{4}$-inch pieces. Heat bacon drippings in a skillet. Sauté okra 10 to 15 minutes, stirring occasionally, until it begins to look dry and loses its ropy texture. Stir in onion and cook until transparent. Add tomatoes and seasonings, including the parsley. Lower heat and continue cooking several minutes. Serve with rice and corn bread for a real down-home meal like mamma used to make.

MARINATED VEGETABLE SALAD

Serves 4

1 (9-ounce) package frozen Brussels sprouts, cooked and drained

2 (14-ounce) cans artichoke hearts, cut in quarters

1 pint cherry tomatoes, halved

4 large ripe avocados, cut in bite-size pieces

1 (10-ounce) can small pitted black olives, drained

1/2 cup fresh parsley, chopped

1 cup Italian salad dressing

Mix the vegetables, avocados, black olives, and parsley in a clear glass salad bowl. Pour the dressing over the vegetables. Toss gently. Cover and chill 1 to 2 hours. This salad is best if not marinated too long. Toss gently before serving. Serve over lettuce leaves.

WILD RICE SALAD

Serves 6

1 (8-ounce) package wild rice
6 ribs celery, chopped
2 large green bell peppers, chopped
2 large red bell peppers, chopped
1 onion, finely chopped
2 to 4 tablespoons fresh lemon juice
3 cloves garlic, minced
1 cup fresh parsley, chopped
Garlic salt to taste
Freshly ground black pepper to taste
Creamy Italian dressing, as needed

Cook wild rice according to directions. Drain and cool. Add the celery, peppers, and onion to the rice, and mix in the lemon juice, seasonings, and enough dressing to bind ingredients. Refrigerate overnight. Adjust seasonings to taste. Serve and enjoy.

CROUTONS WITH PARSLEY

Serves 4

3 slices white bread
3 tablespoons butter
Dash of seasoning salt, or to taste
2 tablespoons minced fresh parsley

Cut the bread into crouton-sized cubes. Melt the butter over medium heat and add the bread cubes and seasoning salt. Cook until light brown. Stir frequently during this process. Stir in the parsley, then remove the croutons and drain on paper towels. Let cool and cover in a container with a tight-fitting lid.

SHRIMP WITH LEMON AND PARSLEY LINGUINE

8 ounces linguine

2 tablespoons cold pressed olive oil

2 tablespoons unsalted butter

3 cloves garlic, minced

1–1½ pounds large shrimp (15 to 20 count)

¼ cup lemon juice

Zest of 1 lemon

¼ teaspoon crushed red pepper

3 tablespoons chopped fresh parsley

¼ teaspoon salt

¼ teaspoon pepper

Cook the pasta according to package directions; cover and keep warm. Heat the olive oil and butter in a large sauté pan over medium heat. Add garlic and sauté briefly, then add shrimp. Cook shrimp on both sides until they turn pink, about 5 minutes. Add the remaining ingredients, turn off the heat, and mix to combine. Add pasta and toss. Serve and enjoy.

HERBED FISH FILETS

Serves 4

4 (1-pound) filets
1/2 teaspoon salt
Dash of garlic powder
1 tablespoon nonfat dry milk
1 tablespoon water
1/4 cup drained, chopped canned mushrooms
1/2 teaspoon onion powder
1/2 teaspoon dried parsley
1/2 teaspoon lemon juice
1/8 teaspoon ground thyme
Dash of black pepper

Preheat oven to 350°F. Sprinkle the fish with salt and garlic powder. Mix the remaining ingredients and spread over fish. Bake for 20 minutes, or until fish flakes with fork.

TIM'S ROAST CHICKEN AND PARSLEY

Serves 4

1 (3- to 4-pound) chicken
Salt and freshly ground black pepper to taste
1/2 cup olive oil
1/4 cup lemon juice
1 teaspoon ground thyme
1 bunch parsley

Preheat oven to 350°F. Wash and dry chicken. Salt and pepper it inside and out. Rub the bird well again, inside and out, with dressing made of the oil, lemon juice, and thyme. Stuff the bird loosely with the fresh parsley and roast, uncovered, for about 1 1/4 hours.

LINGUINE AND CHICKEN IN LEMON PARSLEY SAUCE

Serves 4

Zest of 1 lemon, finely chopped
1 tablespoon olive oil
1 teaspoon finely chopped ginger
1 teaspoon sugar
1 cup chicken broth
8 ounces linguine
2 boneless, skinless chicken breasts, skinned, boned, and cut in cubes
2 shallots, finely chopped
2 tablespoons margarine
3 cups stemmed parsley, chopped
Salt and freshly ground black pepper to taste

Simmer lemon zest in oil in a medium saucepan for 3 to 4 minutes. Add ginger and sugar; cook 3 minutes more. Stir often. Pour in broth; bring to boil. Reduce total liquid to approximately 1/2 cup. Cook linguine until it is al dente. In a skillet cook chicken and shallots in margarine until lightly browned, about 3 minutes. Add lemon sauce mixture, then parsley and cook 3 to 4 minutes more. Season with salt and pepper. Put drained pasta in casserole. Toss chicken sauce with pasta. Let stand 5 minutes to absorb flavors before serving.

SALSA VERDE

Serves 4

1 cup chopped parsley
$^1/_4$ cup chopped green onion
2 tablespoons capers
1 garlic clove, chopped
$^2/_3$ cup mayonnaise
2 tablespoons olive oil
1 tablespoon lemon juice
$^1/_2$ teaspoon prepared mustard

Combine the parsley, green onion, capers, and garlic in blender or food processor. Cover and process until finely chopped. Add remaining ingredients and blend well. Chill. Serve with hot or cold stone crab claws or boiled shrimp. Makes $1^1/_4$ cups sauce.

NEW MEXICAN PIZZA

Makes 4 individual pies

1 pound lean ground beef
2 cloves garlic, minced
1 large green or red bell pepper, diced
2 large tomatoes, chopped
1/2 cup chopped parsley
3 tablespoons tomato paste
1/2 to 1 tablespoon chopped jalapeno pepper
1 teaspoon chili powder
1 teaspoon ground cumin
1 teaspoon dried oregano leaves
1/2 teaspoon ground cinnamon
Salt and pepper to taste
4 wheat tortillas
2 cups shredded Monterey Jack or cheddar cheese
Lettuce, shredded, and tomatoes, chopped, for garnish

Brown beef, garlic, and bell pepper over medium-high heat until meat is no longer pink. Drain and discard fat. Preheat broiler. Add next 8 ingredients plus salt and pepper to meat mixture. Place tortillas on a cookie sheet. Broil 6 inches from heat for 30 seconds per side. Top each tortilla with 1/2 cup meat mixture then 1/2 cup cheese, spread within 1/2-inch of tortilla's edge. Return to broiler until cheese has melted. Garnish with lettuce and tomato and serve.

MEDITERRANEAN CUCUMBERS AND TOMATOES

Serves 4

2 tablespoons olive oil
1 tablespoon apple cider vinegar
1 tablespoon chopped fresh parsley
1 tablespoon chopped fresh basil
1/4 teaspoon salt
1/4 teaspoon freshly ground black pepper
3 medium tomatoes, sliced
1/2 large cucumber, sliced
1 small onion, sliced
Leaf lettuce

In a small bowl, whisk together the oil, vinegar, parsley, basil, salt, and pepper. Arrange the tomatoes, cucumbers, and onions over the lettuce leaves on an attractive serving platter. Drizzle with the vinaigrette and serve.

Bonus Recipe

Okay, so maybe it doesn't have anything to do with parsley, but what decent cookbook from the South could be opened without finding a recipe for pecan pie? Not this one, we assure you! This one on the next page is our favorite, and it makes two pies!

WORLD FAMOUS PECAN PIE

Makes 2 pies

4 large eggs
1 cup white sugar
1 cup dark corn syrup
1 cup white corn syrup
4 tablespoons flour
2 teaspoons pure vanilla extract
4 tablespoons butter, melted
1/2 teaspoon salt
2 unbaked pie shells
2 cups pecan halves

Preheat oven to 350°F. Slightly beat the 4 eggs and add the sugar, syrups, flour, vanilla, butter, and salt. Pour this into pie shells, adding 1 cup pecans to each pie, spreading them around until they are even. Bake for about 45 minutes. Be glad this makes 2 pies, because pecan pie is always a hit!

PARSLEY SAUCE

Serves 4

4 tablespoons butter

6 tablespoons flour

1 1/2 to 2 cups milk, to taste

3 tablespoons fresh parsley, chopped fine

Salt to taste

Melt butter in saucepan; add flour while stirring. Add milk, a little at a time, continually stirring until you reach a good consistency, thick or thin depending on your liking. Milk measurements can be increased or decreased. Add parsley and salt to taste. Serve on Swedish Meatballs (see page 48) or over boiled new potatoes.

NOTES FROM THE KITCHEN

NOTES FROM THE GARDEN

Chapter Sixteen

SAVORY

Well, what is it to be—winter savory or summer savory? In almost any instance the two are the same, the exception being gardening. Can you remember this? Winter savory is a perennial and summer savory an annual. Now that we've established this information, let us get to know this herb better.

Savory likes full sun and a well-drained location. Use fresh seeds as they lose their viability after one year. Sow summer savory seeds in the garden after danger of frost has disappeared. The seeds will sprout quickly. It is also a good idea to soak savory seeds in hot water overnight before planting.

Thin to about 10 inches apart and keep seedlings weeded. As soon as the plants reach about 6 inches tall, snip the top of the branches to harvest. Dry the leaves and place in a jar with a desiccant added.

If you decide to try winter savory, you might find it a little slower to sprout. The plants should be 10 to 12 inches apart. They will prefer less water than their counterpart, as too much water causes winterkill. You can harvest fresh savory all winter if you live in a mild climate. Winter savory will have to be replaced every two or three years.

Savory reproduces vigorously. As a nice gift for a friend, snip off a handful of the spring shoots and place into a container of sandy soil. Savory also does well growing in containers. Their feet enjoy a fast-draining soil, and savory loves a once-a-month feeding.

Both savories are used in the kitchen. Both can be used to marry the various flavors used in recipes. Summer savory has a peppery-thyme taste that blends well in teas, herbal butters, and flavored vinegars. It also goes well with shell beans, lentils, peas, winter root vegetables, any vegetables from the cabbage family, squash, garlic, and various soups. Fresh summer savory leaves can be minced and added with garlic, bay, and freshly squeezed lemon juice as a marinade for fish.

Winter savory has a much stronger taste. It is often used with game meats and potatoes. The leaves are also suitable for soups and stews. The flowers of both savories are used in salads and as a garnish. We have used savory in the following recipes and have found savory to be an interesting herb.

SAVORY RED SAUCE

Serves 4

2 cups peeled, seeded, and chopped tomatoes
2 cloves garlic, minced
1 medium onion, chopped
1 cup water
1 tablespoon minced fresh savory
1 tablespoon minced fresh basil
1 tablespoon minced fresh parsley
1/4 teaspoon salt
1/4 teaspoon freshly ground pepper
4 tablespoons butter
1 tablespoon all-purpose flour

Combine the tomatoes, garlic, onion, water, herbs, salt, and pepper in a saucepan over medium heat. Cook 15 minutes or until vegetables are tender. In a skillet, melt the butter, and add the flour. Cook, stirring constantly for 1 minute. Slowly pour in the tomato mixture, again stirring constantly, and bring to a boil. Reduce heat and simmer for 3 minutes or until thickened. Serve over pasta, or use as a sauce over grilled meat or vegetables.

CHICKEN AND SMOKED SAUSAGE FILÉ GUMBO

Serves 6

4 serving-size pieces chicken
2 teaspoons cajun spice blend
3/4 pound smoked pork sausage, thickly sliced
3 tablespoons vegetable oil
4 tablespoons plain flour
4 ounces lean baked ham, cut into small cubes
2 onions, chopped
1 green pepper, chopped
2 stalks celery, chopped
1 spring onion, thinly sliced
1 tablespoon chopped fresh parsley
2 cloves garlic, finely chopped
1 3/4 pints chicken stock
1 teaspoon sea salt
1 teaspoon crushed black peppercorns
1 teaspoon savory
1/4 teaspoon cayenne pepper
2 crushed bay leaves
3 teaspoons filé powder
4 servings cooked long grain rice (jasmine rice preferably)

Preheat oven to 175°F. Rub chicken pieces with cajun spice blend and set aside. Fry the sausage slices in a heavy casserole dish until they give up some of their fat, 5 to 10 minutes. Drain and set aside. Throw away the fat. Put the vegetable oil in casserole dish and heat until hot but not smoking. Add the chicken and cook until browned all over, about 15 minutes. Drain and keep warm in the oven. Gradually add the flour to the oil, stirring all the time to make a roux. Turn the heat down to low and cook, stirring all the time, until the roux is golden brown, about 15 minutes. Be careful not to burn roux. Mix in the sausage, ham, onions, green pepper, celery, spring onions, parsley, and garlic. Cook for another

10 minutes stirring all the time. Mix 4 tablespoons of the stock together with the chicken, sea salt, ground black peppercorns, savory, cayenne, and bay leaves. Stir well, then gradually add the rest of the stock. Turn up the heat and bring to boiling, then turn heat back down and simmer on reduced heat until the chicken is tender, about an hour, stirring frequently. Remove from heat and let stand for 5 minutes. Stir in the filé powder. Leave for another 5 minutes. Serve with the rice.

SAFFRON RISOTTO

Serves 4

2 tablespoons sugar
4 fluid ounces water
2 fluid ounces rice vinegar
1 lemon, sliced
3-inch piece of cinnamon bark
Handful figs, preferably fresh
1 tablespoon butter
1 onion, finely chopped
About 10 saffron threads
4 servings rice, preferably Arborio
8 fluid ounces dry white wine
2 pints chicken stock
2 ounces freshly grated Parmesan cheese
1/2 teaspoon dried savory
Salt and freshly cracked black pepper to taste

Mix the sugar, water, vinegar, lemon, and cinnamon together in a saucepan and gently simmer for 5 minutes. Add figs and simmer for another 10 minutes. Cover. Let mixture stand 1 hour for flavors to infuse.

Drain, remove the cinnamon and lemon, and coarsely chop the figs. Set aside. Meantime, melt butter in frying pan, stir in onion, and sauté until soft, about 5 minutes. Add saffron and cook for a minute more before stirring in rice. Add wine, and continue stirring until absorbed.

Continue cooking and add the stock a little at a time, continuing to stir until fully absorbed. After about 30 minutes all the stock should be absorbed and the rice should be tender and creamy looking but still al dente. Stir in the figs, Parmesan, thyme, salt, and black pepper and heat through. Serve and enjoy.

Savory Lore

Savory was the favored herb of Europeans until world exploration and trade brought back spices from far away. The Romans used savory extensively in their cooking. Beekeepers often grew savory near their hives to enhance the flavor of their honey. Today, as in the past, crushed savory leaves can be rubbed into insect bites for quick relief.

ASIAN BEAN SALAD

Serves 4

- 1/2 cup adzuki beans
- 1/4 teaspoon salt
- 1 clove garlic, minced
- 4 tablespoons chopped red onion
- 3 tablespoons chopped celery
- 3 tablespoons chopped red bell peppers
- 3 tablespoons blanched and chopped snow peas
- 4 sprigs winter savory, chopped
- 1 tablespoon olive oil
- 1 tablespoon rice wine vinegar
- 1/2 teaspoon fresh lemon juice
- 1/4 teaspoon salt
- 1/4 teaspoon ground cumin
- 1/4 teaspoon toasted sesame oil
- 1/8 teaspoon freshly ground black pepper
- 1/8 teaspoon Asian chili sauce

Cover the beans in four times the volume of 2 cups of water and let soak overnight. Drain off the water and place the beans in a pot. Cover with 5 cups of water; add the salt and garlic. Bring to a boil and cook until the beans are soft but still retain their shape. Remove from heat, drain, and rinse briefly with warm water. When drained, place in a mixing bowl, add the remaining ingredients, and toss gently until everything is evenly blended. Colorful and filled with lively flavors, this salad is a perfect match with grilled chicken or fish.

POULTRY OR FISH STUFFING WITH SAVORY

Serves 4

1 onion, chopped
2 tablespoons butter, melted
2 cups breadcrumbs
3 teaspoons dried or chopped fresh summer savory, or 2 teaspoons of dried or fresh winter savory
Salt and freshly ground black pepper to taste

Sauté the onion in the butter. Mix all ingredients and use as stuffing for poultry or fish, or as a side dish with poultry or fish.

BEANS WITH WINTER SAVORY

Serves 4

3 tablespoons bacon drippings
1 onion, chopped
1 can chicken stock
2 cups dried beans of your choice (navy, pinto, etc.)
1 tablespoon winter savory, dried or chopped fresh
Salt and freshly ground black pepper to taste

Place bacon drippings in pot big enough to cook the beans. Add onion and gently cook, while stirring, until translucent. Add the chicken stock, beans, and savory to the pot, also adding enough water to completely cover the beans. Bring to a boil, then lower heat and simmer for 2 hours, or until the beans are done. Drain and place in a serving bowl, and add salt and pepper as needed.

SAVORY MUSHROOM QUICHE

Makes 1 pie

1 unbaked pastry shell
1 tablespoon butter
4 cups sliced fresh mushrooms
1 small onion, chopped
1 cup shredded Swiss cheese
2 tablespoons all-purpose flour
3 eggs, lightly beaten
1 1/4 cups half-and-half
1 teaspoon dried savory
1/2 teaspoon salt
1/2 teaspoon freshly ground black pepper
1/4 teaspoon nutmeg

Preheat oven to 450°F. Line the unbaked pastry shell into a pie plate and do not pierce the pastry. Line the shell with a double thickness of foil filled with dried beans or aluminum pie weights. Bake for 8 minutes. Remove from oven and set aside. Melt the butter in a skillet, and sauté the mushrooms and onion. Remove with a slotted spoon and set aside.

Reduce oven temperature to 350°F. In a bowl, combine the remaining ingredients. Add the mushrooms and onion; gently stir. Pour the egg mixture into the hot pastry shell and bake for 45 minutes, or until a knife inserted in center comes out clean. Allow to stand 10 minutes before cutting.

SEAFARING LINGUINE

Serves 4

8 ounces linguine
$6^1/2$ cans minced clams
2 tablespoons olive oil
$^1/2$ cup chopped onion
2 cloves garlic, minced
$^1/4$ teaspoon red pepper, crushed
1 teaspoon dried savory, crushed
1 tablespoon dried parsley, crushed
$^1/2$ cup dry white wine
$^1/3$ cup oil-packed dried tomatoes

Cook the pasta al dente and cover to keep warm. Drain the clams, reserving the liquid. Heat olive oil in a saucepan, and cook the onion, garlic, and herbs until onion is tender. Drain off any leftover oil. Add the white wine and the reserved clam juice. Bring to boil, reduce heat, and boil for about 10 minutes. While this is gently boiling, drain the dried tomatoes and cut into strips. Stir the tomatoes and the drained clams into the saucepan. Heat through. Serve the clam mixture over the pasta. Garnish with fresh parsley sprigs.

ELEGANT CHOCOLATE FONDUE

Serves 4

3 tablespoons butter
1/4 cup ground and toasted pecans
6 ounces semi-sweet chocolate, chopped
3 ounces milk chocolate, chopped
1/4 cup heavy cream
1 tablespoon amaretto
Pound cake cut into 1-inch cubes
Assorted fresh fruits, cut into chunks (such as strawberries, kiwi, pineapple, and papaya)

Coat the insides of 6-ounce glass dessert dishes with 2 tablespoons of the butter. Sprinkle the inside of each dish with toasted pecans to form a thin layer. Combine in a heavy saucepan the semi-sweet chocolate, milk chocolate, 1 tablespoon butter, the heavy cream, and the amaretto. Stir over low heat until the chocolate is melted and the mixture is smooth. Carefully spoon the fondue mixture into the coated dessert glasses. Serve warm with the pound cake and the fruits. This dessert is sure to be a hit!

NOTES FROM THE KITCHEN

NOTES FROM THE GARDEN

Chapter Seventeen

FENNEL

Fennel is beautiful growing on the landscape. Its handsome feathery leaves are either purple-bronze or green. The plants will grow up to 3 feet tall, so they make a beautiful backdrop for shorter flowers or herbs.

To grow fennel, buy organically grown plants and place them in an area that allows at least six hours of sun per day. Plant fennel as you would any other plant and be sure to give it a nice drink of water. Water fennel in a drought situation. Some plants are offended by the presence of fennel. They include bush beans, caraway, coriander, kohlrabi, and tomatoes.

A good reason to raise fennel is to attract the swallowtail butterfly caterpillar. Don't be surprised when these green, black, and yellow striped caterpillars show up to enjoy the nectar of the fennel flowers. Be sure to grow enough fennel plants for both you and these soon-to-be beautiful yellow, blue, orange, black, and white butterflies. Any gardener will be pleased to have these guys as guests in their garden. Sir Winston Churchill kept a caged garden of fennel at his estate in England for the very purpose of attracting swallowtail butterflies.

The fennel leaves can be harvested at any time and are best preserved by freezing. The seeds are best harvested as they turn from yellowish-green to brown. The leaves are especially good when paired with salads, dips, sauces, marinades, butters, and vinegars.

They also go nicely with fish, eggs, rice, cheese, and vegetables. The seeds can be used ground or whole, in sausages, cakes, cookies, breads, or fruit desserts. Fennel is also necessary when making a red sauce to go over pasta. Heat will destroy the delicate flavor of fennel leaves, so be sure to add to cooked recipes at the last few moments of cooking.

Don't forget to eat the fennel bulbs, as they are tasty and good for you. Mince a bulb of fennel and add to a salad of grapefruit and avocado. We experimented with fennel to come up with these recipes. Try them in your kitchen to see what you think!

FENNEL PORK CHOPS

Serves 4

4 pork chops

2 tablespoons garlic salt

2 tablespoons olive oil

1 tablespoon fennel seed, or 2 tablespoons fresh fennel, minced

1 cup white wine

Salt and freshly ground black pepper to taste

Sprinkle garlic salt over the pork chops. Heat the olive oil in a pan and add pork chops, sprinkling the fennel over the top. Brown both sides of the pork chops, then add the wine, salt, and pepper and simmer for 10 minutes. Add more wine during this process as necessary. Serve hot.

BAKED MUSHROOMS

Serves 4

- 12 large mushrooms
- 2 tablespoons olive oil
- 1 bunch spring onions, chopped, including some green tops
- 3 cloves garlic, minced
- 1 teaspoon fennel seeds
- 1½ tablespoons dried thyme
- 6 ounces blue cheese, crumbled
- ¼ cup breadcrumbs
- Leaves of 2 fennel bulbs, chopped
- 1 teaspoon freshly squeezed lemon juice
- Salt and freshly ground black pepper to taste

Wipe the mushrooms with a damp cloth to clean. (Never use water to clean mushrooms.) Coarsely chop the stems after removing them from the caps. Set the caps aside. Heat 2 teaspoons olive oil in a sauté pan, and add the spring onions and garlic. Briefly cook, then add the mushroom stems, fennel seeds, and the thyme. Sauté until soft and remove from heat. Allow to cool, Preheat oven to 400°F.

Add cheese, breadcrumbs, chopped fennel leaves, lemon juice, salt, and pepper to the other ingredients. Loosely stuff mushroom caps with filling, mounding it slightly in the middle. Place stuffed caps in shallow baking dish. Drizzle lightly with olive oil. Bake for 10 minutes or until lightly browned. Cool slightly and place on top of the Mixed Greens and Fennel Salad (see recipe on page 210).

MIXED GREENS AND FENNEL SALAD

Serves 4

Salad

- 12 cups mixed green salad (arugula, escarole, endive, romaine, etc.)
- 2 fennel bulbs, trimmed and chopped
- 1/4 cup chopped spring onions
- 1/4 cup salad burnette (if available)
- 1 green pepper, seeded and chopped
- 1 red pepper, seeded and chopped
- 1 tablespoon fresh thyme leaves

Mix greens and vegetables together and garnish with mushroom caps (from previous page).

Dressing

- 6 tablespoons red wine vinegar
- 1 tablespoon freshly squeezed lemon juice
- 1 tablespoon dijon mustard
- 1 tablespoon Italian parsley, chopped
- 2 cloves garlic, minced
- 1/2 teaspoon paprika
- 1/2 cup extra-virgin olive oil

In a small bowl, combine all ingredients except olive oil. Finally, slowly drizzle in olive oil, whisking constantly until emulsified. Drizzle the finished vinaigrette over salad and mushrooms. Your family and guests will adore you for this!

FUSILLI WITH FENNEL

Serves 4

2 tablespoons raisins
$^3/_4$ cup dry white wine
4 large garden tomatoes, or 2 cups canned plum tomatoes
4 tablespoons olive oil
1 large onion, chopped
6 cloves garlic, minced
$^1/_2$ cup pine nuts
2 bay leaves
$^1/_4$ cup chopped fresh oregano
1 pound fusilli
$^3/_4$ cup freshly minced fennel tops
Salt and freshly ground black pepper

Allow the raisins to steep in the wine until softened. Place them in a blender with the tomatoes; puree and set aside. Heat 2 tablespoons of olive oil over moderate heat in a large, heavy saucepan. Sauté the onion and garlic until translucent. Add the pine nuts to this mixture and sauté for 1 minute. Add tomato puree, bay leaves, and oregano. Heat to simmering.

While mixture simmers, bring a large pot of salted water to a boil and add pasta. Meanwhile stir the fennel tops, salt, and pepper into the sauce. The pasta should boil for about 10 minutes, or to desired tenderness. Drain and transfer to a large bowl. Use remaining oil to toss and coat pasta. Remove bay leaves from sauce and pour sauce over pasta. Serve with a salad of mixed greens and some hard crusty bread. Enjoy!

Fennel Lore

Fennel is another one of those herbs that has been of use to mankind for many centuries. Roman soldiers ate it for strength, while the women used it to help keep them thin.

To the Anglo-Saxons, fennel was one of the nine sacred herbs with power over evil. It was mentioned frequently in their cooking and medicinal recipes. By the 1600s people were eating fennel along with fish and meat as an aid to digestion.

Twenty-five miles from Athens, Greece, fennel grew abundantly in a small village. In 490 B.C.E. the Greeks defeated the Persian army. A runner was dispatched to bring the news to Athens. To celebrate the feat of this runner, his hometown's name has become the label for a twenty-six-mile endurance race known as the marathon. Don't you just know that his wife or mother used lots of fennel in her recipes?

MEAT LOAF, ITALIAN STYLE

Serves 4

1 (8-ounce) can pizza sauce
1 egg, slightly beaten
1/2 cup chopped onion
1/2 cup chopped green pepper
1 teaspoon fennel seeds, crushed
1 teaspoon dried oregano
1/4 cup Parmesan cheese
1 pound lean ground beef
Salt and freshly ground black pepper

Preheat oven to 350°F. Open pizza sauce and measure out 1/2 cup. Set aside. In a separate mixing bowl, combine remaining pizza sauce with remaining ingredients. Gently work mixture into a loaf pan. Pour reserved pizza sauce over the top. Bake for 1 hour and 15 minutes.

PORK ROAST WITH FENNEL AND VEGETABLES

Serves 4

4 cloves garlic, minced
1 teaspoon fennel seeds, crushed
1 teaspoon oregano, crushed
1/2 teaspoon freshly ground black pepper
Salt to taste
1 (2 to 2 1/2 pounds) boneless pork shoulder roast
2 tablespoons olive oil
2 pounds small red potatoes, washed and halved
1 fennel bulb, trimmed and sliced into 1-inch pieces
1 medium onion, sliced

Preheat the oven to 350°F. Combine the garlic with fennel seeds, oregano, pepper, and salt in a small bowl. Trim fat from meat and rub the seasoning mixture over the roast. Heat olive oil in a Dutch oven. Brown the roast on all sides. Arrange the potatoes, fennel, and onion in a large baking dish. Sprinkle with remaining herbs. Pour 1/2 cup water over the vegetables. Nestle the roast on the top of the vegetables. Cover and bake 1 hour and 15 minutes, or until meat thermometer registers 170°F.

HERBED TOMATO SAUCE

Serves 4

2 tablespoons olive oil
2 medium onions, chopped
4 cloves garlic, minced
2 (16-ounce) cans tomatoes
1 (6-ounce) can tomato paste
2 cups fresh mushrooms, sliced
2 tablespoons Parmesan cheese, grated
2 teaspoons dried oregano, crushed
2 teaspoons dried basil, crushed
1 teaspoon fennel seeds, crushed
1 teaspoon brown sugar
1 teaspoon salt
1/2 teaspoon crushed red pepper

Heat olive oil in a large skillet. Add onions and garlic. Sauté until tender. Add tomatoes and tomato paste. Combine thoroughly. Add remaining ingredients. Simmer at least 1 hour. This sauce can be used over any pasta that has been cooked and drained.

FENNEL SALAD

Serves 4

8 medium fennel bulbs, washed and trimmed
3 navel oranges, peeled and sectioned
3 lemons, peeled and sectioned
1/3 cup olive oil
2 teaspoons salt
2 teaspoons coriander seeds
1/2 teaspoon freshly ground black pepper
3 tomatoes, peeled, seeded, and diced
1/2 cup black niçoise olives in brine, pitted and halved
1/3 cup pine nuts
Feta cheese, to taste, crumbled

Halve the fennel bulbs lengthwise. Remove the tough cores. Thinly slice the fennel bulbs crosswise. Spread in a flat serving dish. Set aside. Place orange sections, lemon sections, olive oil, salt, coriander seeds, and pepper in a blender. Puree until smooth. Cook the tomatoes together with the mixture from blender over low heat in a medium saucepan until warm. To serve, pour warm dressing over the sliced fennel and toss gently. Sprinkle olives, pine nuts, and feta cheese on top.

TIM AND JAN'S MINESTRONE

Serves 4

3 bacon slices, diced
1 tablespoon olive oil
1 large onion, peeled and diced
4 cloves garlic, minced
1 carrot, scraped and diced
2 small zucchini, washed, trimmed, and chopped
1 (16-ounce) can tomatoes, undrained and chopped
2 cups potatoes, peeled and diced
8 cups chicken stock
2 teaspoons salt
1 teaspoon freshly ground black pepper
1 teaspoon fennel seeds, crushed
1 (16-ounce) can kidney beans, drained
1 cup small pasta (such as ditalini or orzo), uncooked
1/2 cup Parmesan cheese

Combine the bacon, olive oil, onions, and garlic in a large saucepan. Cook over low heat until tender. Add the carrot and cook another 5 minutes. Add the zucchini, tomatoes, potatoes, chicken stock, salt, pepper, and fennel seeds. Bring to a boil. Reduce heat and simmer, covered, for 25 minutes. Add beans and pasta. Cook another 15 minutes or until pasta is tender. Serve in soup bowls with Parmesan cheese sprinkled over the top.

CHICKEN MANICOTTI WITH ROASTED RED BELL PEPPER SAUCE

Serves 4

1 (8-ounce) package manicotti shells
4 cups cooked chicken, finely chopped
1 (10-ounce) package frozen chopped spinach, thawed and well drained
2 (8-ounce) containers chive-and-onion cream cheese, softened
1/2 cup Italian-seasoned breadcrumbs
4 cloves garlic, minced
1 cup shredded mozzarella cheese
1 teaspoon freshly ground black pepper
1 teaspoon salt
1 teaspoon fennel seeds, crushed
2 teaspoons dried basil, crushed
Cooking spray

Cook pasta according to package instructions. Drain and set aside. In a separate bowl, stir together cooked chicken, spinach, cream cheese, breadcrumbs, garlic, mozzarella cheese, and remaining seasonings. Gently work chicken mixture into pasta tubes, being careful not to tear shells. Place stuffed shells in 2 lightly sprayed 11 x 7-inch baking dishes. Make Roasted Red Bell Pepper Sauce (page 219) and proceed with recipe.

ROASTED RED BELL PEPPER SAUCE

Serves 4

2 (7-ounce) jars roasted red bell peppers, drained

1 (16-ounce) jar creamy Alfredo sauce

3-ounce package shredded Parmesan cheese

Fresh parsley, chopped

$^{1}/_{3}$ cup pine nuts, for garnish, optional

Preheat oven to 350°F. Process bell peppers, Alfredo sauce, and cheese in a blender until smooth. Chicken Manicotti (page 218). Bake for 30 minutes. Garnish with parsley and pine nuts if desired.

MARINATED OLIVES

Serves 4

$1^1/_2$ cups black and green olives
1 cup olive oil
3 cloves garlic, minced
2 bay leaves, crushed
2 teaspoons fennel seeds
2 (1-inch-wide) strips lemon peel
1 teaspoon red pepper flakes

Soak the olives in fresh water for an hour to remove some of the salt. Drain. Set aside. Combine the olive oil, garlic, bay leaves, fennel seeds, lemon strips, and red pepper flakes in a glass measuring cup. Mix thoroughly. Pour over the olives and stir to distribute the marinade. Store covered in refrigerator. These olives should be allowed to marinate for several days before serving. Remove from refrigerator an hour before serving so the oil liquefies. Use as a garnish or make-ahead appetizer.

EGGPLANT PARMESAN

Serves 4

2 medium eggplants, washed and stemmed
Salt
1 cup olive oil
1 medium onion, chopped
3 cloves garlic, minced
1 medium tomato, peeled, seeded, and chopped
1 (6-ounce) can tomato paste
1 cup water
1 teaspoon dried basil, crushed
1 teaspoon dried oregano, crushed
1 teaspoon fennel seeds, crushed
$^1/_2$ teaspoon salt
$^1/_2$ teaspoon freshly ground black pepper
1 cup unbleached all-purpose flour
2 eggs, slightly beaten
$^3/_4$ pound mozzarella cheese, sliced
1 cup Parmesan cheese, grated

Slice eggplants crosswise into $^1/_4$-inch-thick slices. Place in a colander and sprinkle with salt. Allow to drain for 30 minutes. Use paper towel to wipe the slices dry. Heat 2 tablespoons olive oil in a large skillet. Sauté the onions and garlic until tender. Add the tomato, tomato paste, water, herbs, salt, and pepper. Cook slowly, uncovered, for about 30 minutes, stirring occasionally. Place the flour on a plate. Dredge eggplant slices through flour, then through beaten egg. Heat more of the olive oil in another skillet, adding as needed. Sauté eggplant slices until tender. Drain on paper towels.

Preheat oven to 350°F. Place some of the eggplant in bottom of a 13 x 9-inch baking dish. Layer several mozzarella cheese slices over eggplant. Pour some of the sauce over this. Sprinkle with Parmesan cheese. Continue layering, ending with Parmesan cheese. Bake for 30 minutes, or until hot and bubbly. Let stand for 5 to 10 minutes before serving.

CONFETTI RICE

Serves 4

1 (10-ounce) package frozen green peas
2 cups cooked rice
2 tablespoons chopped pimento
2/3 cup olive oil
4 tablespoons red wine vinegar
1/2 teaspoon salt
1/2 teaspoon ground white pepper
1/2 teaspoon fennel seeds
1/4 teaspoon sugar
1/2 teaspoon dried basil, crushed
Lettuce leaves, for serving

Cook peas according to directions. Drain. Combine peas with rice and pimentos. Stir well. Combine oil, vinegar, and seasonings in a separate bowl. Stir well. Pour over rice mixture. Stir gently to combine. Cover and refrigerate several hours before serving. Remove from refrigerator and drain. Serve rice on a bed of lettuce leaves.

GRILLED FENNEL

Serves 4

4 tablespoons olive oil, divided
4 fennel bulbs, cut into halves, cores removed
Salt and freshly cracked black pepper, to taste

Brush a grill, over medium heat, with some of the olive oil to prevent fennel from sticking during cooking. Place fennel bulbs cut side down on grill and brush with oil. Season with salt and pepper. Grill for about 2 minutes per side or until limp. Serve as a side dish with your favorite grilled entree for a "change of taste."

BERRY VANILLA TART

Makes 1 tart

- ¾ cup unsalted butter, softened
- ½ cup confectioners' sugar
- 1½ cups all-purpose flour
- 1 package vanilla baking chips, melted and cooled
- ¼ cup heavy cream
- 1 (8-ounce) package cream cheese, softened
- ½ cup orange juice
- ¼ cup sugar
- ½ teaspoon lemon juice
- 1 tablespoon cornstarch
- 1 pint fresh strawberries
- 1 cup fresh blueberries
- 1 cup fresh raspberries

Preheat oven to 300°F. Cream together the butter and confectioners' sugar with electric mixer. Beat in the flour (mixture will become crumbly). Pat into a 12-inch springform pan. Bake until lightly browned, 25 to 28 minutes. Cool. Beat the melted vanilla chips and heavy cream in another mixing bowl. Add the cream cheese and beat until smooth. Spread this over prepared crust. Chill for 30 minutes.

Combine the orange juice, sugar, lemon juice, and cornstarch in saucepan. Bring to a boil over medium heat and boil for 2 minutes, or until thickened, stirring constantly. Remove sauce from heat and allow to cool. Arrange berries in attractive design on the tart. Brush the fruits with the prepared sauce. Chill for at least one hour before serving. Store unused portion in the refrigerator. (If there is any left!)

NOTES FROM THE KITCHEN

NOTES FROM THE GARDEN

Chapter Eighteen

GARLIC

Garlic is undoubtedly one of our favorite herbs. It seems to come up quite often when we are testing recipes. Evidently many other people feel the same way about this popular herb, for history is rich in the use of garlic. Around the world many cultures have long celebrated garlic for its strength-giving properties.

For example, the Chinese herbalists of long ago, as well as today, prescribed chewing garlic to ward off colds and coughs. It has even been reported that Chinese prisoners are required to eat raw garlic each morning to enhance their health and to keep them energized and able to work!

Egyptian slaves were fed garlic and onions to give them the necessary vitality needed to construct the pyramids. Once the Israelites escaped Egyptian bondage, they later stated a longing for the herb in their wilderness wanderings. The ancient Egyptians so highly prized garlic that citizens of the time swore their vows on a bulb of it. In an ancient Egyptian medical textbook, twenty-two health problems that are listed recommend garlic as the cure. Among these were heart ailments, bites, headaches, worms, and tumors. No wonder it was and still is such a popular herb!

Garlic is the main ingredient in the legendary "Four Thieves Vinegar." During a plague that swept through Marseilles, France, four unfortunate condemned thieves were assigned to collect dead bodies for burial.

These men were able to carry out their mission without contracting the dreaded disease by drinking mashed garlic steeped in vinegar. If you travel to France today, you can still buy "Four Thieves Vinegar."

Locate a place in the garden that gets at least six hours of sun each day. The garlic cloves should be planted about 4 inches apart and 2 inches deep. Cover the cloves with soil, and tamp down. Then soak with water.

Fresh garlic is widely available in the grocery store, but try growing some yourself for fun. With the arrival of fall, purchase some organically grown bulbs of garlic from the grocery store. Separate the bulbs into individual cloves. The next summer, cut off the stalks to allow the plant's energy to go into making the bulbs tastier. Don't toss the stalks, as you can chop them to use as you would chives.

When fall comes around again, harvest the bulbs, allowing them a few days to relax. You can then enjoy your own homegrown garlic. You may be thinking this sure sounds like a long time. Well, yes it does, but you will be richly rewarded when you taste the difference between store-bought and homegrown.

Garlic is also useful in the garden as a companion for roses, cabbage, eggplant, tomatoes, and fruit trees. White flies hate garlic as do some other insects. Make a spray of garlic to ward off these predators. Soak 1/4 cup minced or mashed garlic in a quart of water overnight, then strain. Most bugs will be highly insulted and look for a new home. It has also been noted that a garlic spray will keep hungry deer away from tender saplings. Our favorite place to use garlic is in the kitchen. You may recall the chapter about basil and our recipe for our "Essence." Garlic plays an important role in making that "Essence." You could change the herb combination or even add other herbs to it. However, it just would not come together without the garlic! Garlic will enliven so many foods. Try some with eggs, cheese, beef, pork, fish, soups, salads, stews, vegetables, salad dressings, stir-fries, sauces, butters, and marinades.

When cooking garlic, be sure to keep your nose alert to any aroma changes, since garlic becomes bitter when it is burned. For that reason, we always add our garlic close to the end of the recipe. Long, moist cooking, such as in soups and stews, will soften the flavor of garlic. The following are our favorite recipes and we hope they will become yours!

LINGUINE WITH FRESH HERBS

Serves 6

- 3 tablespoons plus 1 teaspoon extra-virgin olive oil
- 1 cup fresh breadcrumbs made from cubed Italian or French bread, including crust, coarsely ground in food processor or blender
- 1/2 cup finely chopped red onion
- 2 teaspoons minced garlic
- 3/4 cup chicken broth, homemade or canned
- 1/2 teaspoon coarse salt
- 1/2 teaspoon red pepper flakes, crushed
- 1/2 cup loosely packed fresh basil leaves, chopped
- 1/3 cup loosely packed fresh mint leaves, chopped
- 1/2 cup loosely packed Italian parsley leaves, chopped
- 3 tablespoons fresh thyme, minced
- 1 pound linguine

Heat 1 teaspoon oil in a nonstick skillet over medium heat. Add the breadcrumbs and toast until golden, stirring frequently to prevent scorching. Remove from heat and transfer to a small bowl. In same skillet, heat remaining 3 tablespoons oil over low heat. Add onion and sauté, stirring frequently, until soft but not brown, about 2 minutes. Add the garlic and cook until soft, about 30 seconds. Stir in the chicken broth and simmer until heated. Season with the salt and red pepper flakes. Transfer mixture to pasta bowl, add fresh herbs, and stir to combine. Cook pasta in 6 quarts boiling water with 2 teaspoons coarse salt until al dente. Drain pasta, transfer to pasta bowl, and toss with herb mixture. Sprinkle toasted breadcrumbs on top and serve.

ROAST LEG OF LAMB WITH GARLIC, LEMON, AND PARSLEY DRESSING

Serves 8

Roast Leg of Lamb

1 ($3^1/_2$- to 4-pound) leg of lamb

1 tablespoon butter

4 to 5 potatoes, peeled and sliced

$1^1/_4$ cups rich chicken stock

Salt and freshly ground pepper, to taste

Garlic, Lemon, and Parsley Dressing

6 cloves garlic, finely chopped or pressed

6 tablespoons finely chopped fresh parsley

6 tablespoons fresh breadcrumbs from white bread whirled in blender

6 tablespoons softened butter

Juice of 1 lemon

Salt and freshly ground black pepper, to taste

Preheat oven to 400°F. Have your butcher trim and tie the leg of lamb. Butter a shallow ovenproof casserole or gratin dish just large enough to hold the lamb comfortably. Arrange potatoes in the bottom of the dish in overlapping rows. Salt and pepper them generously. Place lamb on potatoes and pour in chicken stock. Season generously with salt and pepper. Roast lamb for 25 minutes per pound, or until lamb is pink and tender. If you prefer lamb well done, increase time to 30 minutes per pound.

Meanwhile, make a smooth paste of the garlic, parsley, breadcrumbs, butter, and lemon juice and season with salt and pepper. One hour before the lamb is done, remove it from oven and allow to cool for 15 minutes. Spread the lamb with dressing to cover surface of roast. Return the lamb to oven and bake for remaining hour.

GARLICKY CLAMS WITH LINGUINE

Serves 6

2 tablespoons olive oil
2 dozen littleneck clams, cleaned and scrubbed
1/2 cup finely chopped onions
2 tablespoons chopped garlic
1/4 cup dry white wine
1 pound linguine, cooked al dente
2 tablespoons finely chopped fresh parsley leaves
Additional olive oil, for serving
Salt and freshly ground black pepper to taste

Heat the olive oil in a large sauté pan with a lid over medium heat. When the oil is hot, add the clams. Season with salt and pepper. Cover and sauté for 6 to 8 minutes. Add the onions, garlic, and wine. Continue to sauté for 2 minutes or until the shells completely open. Discard any shells that do not open! Add the cooked pasta. Season with salt and pepper. Continue to sauté for 2 minutes. Add the parsley and mix well. Serve on a large platter. Drizzle with olive oil and serve.

LETTUCE SALAD WITH GARLIC-INFUSED DRESSING

Serves 4

Lettuce Salad

1 large bunch red leaf lettuce, washed and torn
1 large bunch green leaf lettuce, washed and torn
1/2 pound fresh mushrooms, cleaned and sliced
1 small purple onion, thinly sliced
2 dozen cherry tomatoes, washed
1 salad cucumber, peeled and sliced

Place salad ingredients in large pretty bowl. Toss with the following dressing.

Garlic-Infused Dressing

1/2 cup red wine vinegar
1/2 cup extra-virgin olive oil
1/4 cup water
2 teaspoons lemon juice
1 teaspoon sugar
1 teaspoon dijon mustard
1 teaspoon Worcestershire sauce
1 clove garlic, minced

Place ingredients in a small saucepan, over low heat. Heat only enough to warm and combine. Pour dressing over salad just before serving. This is a different twist on salad, but it sure is good!

GARLIC STIR-FRY

Serves 4

2 tablespoons extra-virgin olive oil
3 small yellow squash, sliced
3 small zucchinis, sliced
3 tablespoons fresh basil, chopped
1 clove garlic, minced
Salt and freshly ground black pepper to taste
1/4 cup grated Parmesan cheese

Heat the olive oil in a skillet over medium heat. Add the squash, zucchini, 2 tablespoons of the basil, and the garlic. Stir-fry this for about 5 minutes, until the squash becomes transparent. At this point, season with salt and pepper. Remove from heat and sprinkle with cheese and remaining 1 tablespoon of basil. This is a great little stir-fry to serve alongside almost any meat.

ROASTED GARLIC AND POTATO SOUFFLE

Serves 8

$^1/_2$ cup sliced green onion

$^1/_4$ cup butter, melted

$^1/_4$ cup all-purpose flour

Salt and freshly ground black pepper to taste

2 cups mashed potatoes

$^1/_2$ bulb roasted garlic

1 (8-ounce) carton sour cream

4 large eggs, separated

1 teaspoon dried thyme

1 teaspoon dried chives

Preheat oven to 350°F. Sauté the onions in butter in a large pan over medium-high heat until tender, and then reduce heat to medium. Add the flour and stir until blended. Cook until thick and bubbly. Stir in the salt and pepper, and remove from heat. Stir in the potatoes, garlic, and sour cream. Beat the egg yolks until thick and pale. Gradually stir about a quarter of the hot mixture into the yolks to temper them. Then add the remaining hot mixture, stirring constantly. Beat the egg whites in a large bowl at high speed with an electric mixer until stiff peaks form; gently fold the beaten egg whites into potato mixture. Spoon into a buttered $1^1/_2$-quart soufflé dish. Bake, uncovered, for 40 minutes or until set. Remove and serve immediately.

CREAMED SWEET POTATOES WITH GARLIC AND THYME

Serves 4

8 sweet potatoes, peeled and cut into chunks
3 tablespoons butter or margarine
1 small onion, chopped
1 clove garlic, minced
1 cup milk
1 teaspoon dried thyme
1 teaspoon salt and freshly ground black pepper to taste

Bring the sweet potatoes to a boil in an appropriate pot, then reduce heat and let simmer until tender. Drain and set aside. In the same pot, melt the butter, then add onion and garlic. Cook until golden brown, stirring frequently, for about 5 minutes. Remove pot from heat, return the potatoes, and add the remaining ingredients. Mash until smooth.

NOTES FROM THE KITCHEN

NOTES FROM THE GARDEN

Chapter Nineteen

GINGER

The lemon-spice flavor of ginger adapts to both sweet and savory foods. Seldom does a stir-fry dish start without it. Fresh ginger is found in the cuisines of China, Japan, Southeast Asia, India, and the Caribbean.

Those strange-looking rhizomes found in the grocery store are an easy way to obtain ginger. However, the pale yellow flesh becomes fibrous with age. It may be best to grow your own ginger. Purchase some ginger in the grocery store, and lay it flat in a 1-inch-deep container filled with a fast-drying potting soil.

The best time of year to do this is in early spring, keeping it indoors until all danger of frost has passed. Allow the potted ginger to receive at least six hours of sun each day. The bamboo-like stems and leaves should appear in about ten days. Once the ginger is moved outdoors, be sure to feed it monthly during the growing season with a balanced fertilizer.

After about eight months of growth, the ginger is ready to harvest. Pull the plants out of the container and cut off the leaf stalks. The leaves are very aromatic and may be used as a garnish, or minced to use in spicy soups and salads.

The rhizomes need to be washed and dried. Choose one of the following methods to preserve the ginger. The rhizomes can be peeled and cut into pieces, then placed in a glass jar filled with vodka. This can be kept in the refrigerator for several months. The other method is to wrap the rhizomes in a paper towel and store them in an airtight container in the refrigerator.

You may decide that since the tropical appearance of the plant is so lovely, you prefer to purchase your ginger at the grocery store and keep the plant!

Ginger can really zip up a dish with its wonderfully spicy and lemony flavor. A nice way to experiment with it is to add some ginger to a favorite chili recipe. A teaspoon of freshly grated ginger could be added to enhance the flavor. A quarter of a teaspoon of freshly grated ginger can be added to 2 cups of fresh fruit such as peaches, plums, apricots, or strawberries. In our kitchen, we have been experimenting with ginger and have come up with some delightful recipes. Try these in your kitchen and see what you think.

CHICKEN STIR-FRY

Serves 4

2 tablespoons peanut oil
1 clove garlic, minced
1 tablespoon freshly grated ginger
2 boneless, skinless chicken breasts, cubed
1 cup chopped green onions
1 green pepper, chopped
1 red pepper, chopped
1/4 cup bamboo shoots
Soy sauce to taste
1 tablespoon cornstarch
1/4 cup cold water

In a wok, heat peanut oil until it is almost smoking. Add the garlic, ginger, and chicken. Stir-fry until cooked. With slotted spoon, remove the chicken. Add the onion, peppers, and bamboo shoots. Sprinkle soy sauce to your liking over vegetables. Stir-fry until tender. Return the chicken to the wok and heat through. In a small bowl, mix water with cornstarch. Add this to the wok to thicken. Cook another 3 minutes. Serve this chicken over stir-fry gingered rice (see following page).

GINGER RICE

Follow directions for making white or brown rice, only add 1 tablespoon minced ginger for a nice twist. This is pleasant to serve with a number of different dishes, such as the previous chicken stir-fry recipe.

PECAN MELTAWAYS

Serves 4

1 cup unsalted butter, softened (always use real butter)
1/2 cup sugar
1 tablespoon vanilla extract
2 cups unbleached all-purpose flour
3/4 cup ground pecans, toasted
1 cup confectioners' sugar
1 tablespoon ground nutmeg

Preheat oven to 300°F. Cream the butter, sugar, and vanilla in a large mixing bowl. Gradually add the flour and mix well. Stir in pecans. Shape into 1-inch balls and place on an ungreased cookie sheet. Bake until the bottoms are slightly browned. Allow cookies to cool on wire racks. Combine the confectioners' sugar with the ground nutmeg. Once the cookies have cooled, gently roll them in the sugar mixture. These are so good and your family will be proud of you for making them!

GINGERBREAD WITH WALNUT SAUCE

Serves 8

Gingerbread

1 cup unsalted butter, softened
1 cup sugar
1 cup molasses
2 eggs
3 cups unbleached all-purpose flour
$1^1/_2$ teaspoons salt
$1^1/_2$ teaspoons baking soda
1 teaspoon ground cinnamon
1 teaspoon ground ginger
1 cup hot water

Preheat oven to 350°F. Combine the first four ingredients in a large mixing bowl. Combine the dry ingredients in another mixing bowl. Add the dry mixture to molasses mixture alternately with the hot water. Pour into a greased 13 x 9 x 2-inch baking pan. Bake for 35 to 40 minutes. Cool on wire rack about 10 minutes before releasing from the pan. Serve warm with the following Walnut Sauce recipe.

Walnut Sauce

1 cup packed dark brown sugar

1/2 cup heavy cream

1/4 cup corn syrup

2 tablespoons unsalted butter

1/2 cup chopped walnuts

1 teaspoon pure vanilla extract

Combine the sugar, cream, syrup, and butter in a heavy saucepan. Bring to a boil, stirring constantly. Reduce heat and continue to cook and stir for 5 minutes longer. Remove from heat and stir in the walnuts and vanilla. Spoon over warm gingerbread at serving time. What a nice way to end a meal.

GINGER AND PEAR MUFFINS

Makes 12

$1^1/2$ cups any bran-nugget cereal
$^1/2$ cup pear juice (use apple if not available)
1 pear, coarsely grated
$2^1/2$ teaspoons freshly grated ginger
$^1/2$ cup vanilla yogurt
$^1/4$ cup apple butter
$^1/3$ cup pure maple syrup
2 large eggs
1 tablespoon olive or canola oil
$1^1/2$ cups unbleached all-purpose flour
2 teaspoons baking soda
1 teaspoon ground cinnamon

Preheat oven to 400°F. Combine the first four ingredients in a medium mixing bowl, allowing them to soak for about 10 minutes. Next, stir in the yogurt, apple butter, maple syrup, eggs, and oil. Combine the flour, baking soda, and cinnamon in another mixing bowl. Add the wet ingredients to the flour mixture by pouring into the center and gently mixing with a soft spatula. Do not overmix. Once the ingredients have been combined, pour into lightly greased muffin tins. Bake 18 to 20 minutes.These healthful muffins are great for breakfast or a snack.

TIM'S FRESH GINGER ALE

Makes about 4 quarts

2 cups (about 10 ounces) coarsely chopped, peeled fresh ginger
3 strips lemon peel (about 4 inches each), yellow part only
4 cups water
1 1/2 cups sugar
3 quarts chilled club soda
Ice cubes

Combine the ginger, lemon peel, and water in a 3- to 4-quart pan. Bring to a boil over high heat; boil gently, uncovered, 10 minutes. Stir in the sugar and continue boiling until mixture is reduced to 3 cups, about 15 minutes longer. Pour the mixture through a fine wire strainer set over a bowl. Discard peel; reserve ginger for another use or discard. Cool syrup, cover, and chill until cold, at least 1 hour or up to 1 week.

Mix 1/4 cup of the ginger syrup with 1 cup cold club soda in a 16-ounce glass for each serving. Add more ginger syrup, ice, and sugar to taste. Note: Refrigerate leftover cooked ginger, if desired, and stir into softened vanilla ice cream, or sprinkle over vanilla yogurt or sliced bananas.

GINGERED CHICKEN WITH MANGO

Serves 4

1/4 cup olive oil
2 cloves fresh garlic, crushed
4 boneless, skinless chicken breasts
1 cup peeled and diced mangoes
1/4 cup dark brown sugar
1/4 teaspoon freshly ground cloves
2 teaspoons ground ginger
1/4 teaspoon freshly ground nutmeg
1 teaspoon soy sauce
Salt and freshly ground pepper to taste

Heat the oil in a heavy frying pan. Add the garlic and sauté for a few minutes. Then add chicken filets. Cook for about 15 to 20 minutes, or until chicken is cooked through. Combine the mango with the sugar, cloves, ginger, and nutmeg in a medium-sized bowl. Pour the mixture over the cooked filets and gently mix to cover the chicken pieces. Add soy sauce, salt, and pepper to taste. Cook for about 10 more minutes. Serve hot with a fresh green vegetable and a side dish of rice.

NOTES FROM THE KITCHEN

NOTES FROM THE GARDEN

Chapter Twenty

ENTERTAINING WITH HERBS

Complete Menus and Shopping Lists for Full Course Meals

Entertaining for friends and family is a great way to show off your culinary skills and create exquisite cuisine with these herb recipes. Included in this chapter are complete menus and shopping lists to help you prepare and plan the next event you host. We enjoy using these complete menus for our parties. Hopefully, you will too!

A TERRIFIC TIME WITH TARRAGON

Menu

1. Braised Pork Loin Stuffed with Cheese and Mushrooms (page 74)
2. Raisin and Almond Pilaf (page 76)
3. Asparagus with Tarragon Butter Sauce (page 80)
4. Tarragon Tasty Rolls (page 81)
5. White Chocolate Fruit Torte (page 82)

Personal Shopping List

Meats:

5- to 6-pound boneless pork loin roast

Produce:

1 bunch asparagus

1 bunch tarragon

3 cloves garlic

Handful of shiitake mushrooms

1 red onion

1 pint strawberries

2 kiwis

Dry and Canned Goods:

2 (16-ounce) cans chicken stock

1 (20-ounce) can pineapple chucks

1 (11-ounce) can mandarin oranges

Dairy:

1 egg

1 pound unsalted butter

4 ounces gorgonzola cheese

1 (8-ounce package) cream cheese

4 ounces heavy cream

1 package active yeast

Spice List:

Dried parsley

Dried tarragon

Oregano flakes

Celery seed

Salt and freshly ground black pepper

Fresh tarragon

Other:

Lemon juice

Olive oil

Flour

Cornstarch

Sugar

Confectioners' sugar

10 ounces white chocolate

4 ounces raisins

4 ounces slivered almonds

8 ounces brown rice

8 ounces white chardonnay wine

4 ounces white wine

SUNDOWN WITH SEÑOR AND SEÑORITA CILANTRO

Menu

1. Chicken Cilantro (page 67)
2. Cucumber Lime Salsa (page 68)
3. Rice and Beans with Vinaigrette (page 69)
4. Blueberry Crisp (page 70)

Personal Shopping List

Meats:

4 boneless, skinless chicken breasts

Produce:

1 lime

1 lemon

1 green pepper

1 red pepper

1 large cucumber

1 jalapeno pepper

4 spring onions

3 cloves garlic

1 bunch parsley

1 bunch cilantro

Dry and Canned Goods:

1 (16-ounce) can black beans

Dairy:

4 ounces Monterey Jack cheese

8 ounces unsalted butter

Frozen:

1 (24-ounce) package blueberries (or use fresh blueberries if available)

Spice List:

Ground cumin

Salt and freshly ground black pepper

Coriander seeds

Other:

Olive oil

Honey

Sugar

1 (8-ounce) package blue corn tortilla chips

1 (16-ounce) jar salsa

1 (16-ounce) package long grain rice

All-purpose flour

Red wine vinegar

Brown sugar

THYME TO GATHER AROUND THE TABLE

Menu

1. Thyme-Seasoned Leg of Lamb (page 129)
2. Thyme for Artichoke Salad (page 130)
3. Roasted Garlic and Potato Souffle (page 236)
4. Harvest Pumpkin Cheesecake (page 131)

Personal Shopping List

Meats:

1 6½-pound leg of lamb, butterflied

Produce:

1 bunch green onions

5 cloves garlic

1 bunch parsley

5 pounds potatoes

1 bunch chives

Mixed salad greens (enough for 6 cups)

1 large tomato

1 red onion

Dry and Canned Goods:

1 can sweetened condensed milk

1 can pure pumpkin

1 can black olives

Dairy:

8 ounces unsalted butter

1 (8-ounce) container sour cream

1 dozen eggs

3 (8-ounce) packages cream cheese

Spice List:

Dried basil

Dried thyme

Dried chives

Dried rosemary

Dried tarragon

Salt and freshly ground black pepper

Nutmeg

Ground cinnamon

Prepared mustard

Other:

All-purpose flour

Sugar

Maple syrup

Olive oil

Red wine vinegar

1 (20-ounce) package graham cracker crumbs

4 ounces slivered almonds

4 ounces pecans

1 (6-ounce) jar marinated artichoke hearts

1 loaf white bread

AN EVENING WITH BASIL

Menu

1. Creamy Bacon and Mushroom Sauce with Linguine (page 14)
2. Herbal Italian Dressing (page 16)
3. Basil and Garlic Spread (page 17)
4. Essence (page 15)
5. Tropical Fru Frus (page 18)

Personal Shopping List

Meats:

$1^1/_2$ pounds bacon

Produce:

1 head iceberg lettuce

1 bunch parsley

12 cloves garlic

1 bunch green onions

Handful of mushrooms

Dry and Canned Goods:

1 (8-ounce) can crushed pineapple

1 (8-ounce) can chicken stock

Dairy:

1 (8-ounce) container cream cheese

8 ounces unsalted butter

4 ounces Parmesan cheese

1 (8-ounce) container heavy cream

Spice List:

Lemon basil leaves

Mustard

Freshly ground black pepper

Basil

Sea salt

Other:

Mayonnaise

1 jar maraschino cherries

4 ounces pecans

Shredded coconut

Red wine vinegar

Olive oil

4 ounces white wine

1 (12-ounce) box linguine

TALK IT UP WITH CHIVES

Menu

1. Creamy Chive Butter (page 90)
2. Chicken and Vegetable Papillote (page 92)
3. Chive Muffins (page 93)
4. Chocolate Mousse Soufflé (page 94)

Personal Shopping List

Meats:

4 boneless, skinless chicken breasts

Produce:

1 lemon

1 clove garlic

1 bunch parsley

Dairy:

8 ounces sweet butter

4 eggs

8 ounces buttermilk

8 ounces heavy cream

Frozen:

1 bag mixed vegetable (we suggest carrots, green onions, zucchini, or yellow squash, and green bell pepper)

Spices:

Salt and freshly ground black pepper

Almond extract

Cream of tartar

Baking powder

Other:

Olive oil

Parchment paper

Loaf of crusty bread

All-purpose flour

Sugar

Brown sugar

4 ounces semi-sweet chocolate

AN EVENT WITH OREGANO

Menu

1. Chicken (or Veal) Parmesan (page 45)
2. Romaine and Radicchio Italian Salad (page 47)
3. Dill Butter with Garlic (page 29)
4. Heard it Through the Grapevine (page 53)

Personal Shopping List

Meats:

1 pound chicken or veal

Produce:

1 pound romaine
1 pound radicchio
1 red onion
1 bunch parsley
1 bunch oregano
Handful of cherry tomatoes
2 large onions
6 cloves garlic
2 pounds red or white grapes

Dry and Canned Goods:

1 can black olives
2 (16-ounce) cans tomatoes
1 (8-ounce) can tomato sauce
1 (6-ounce) can tomato paste

Dairy:

1 egg
8 ounces mozzarella cheese
8 ounces unsalted butter

Spice List:

Salt and pepper

Oregano

Basil

Fennel seeds

Sea salt

Other:

4 ounces dried breadcrumbs

Olive oil

4 ounces raisins

White wine

Sugar

Loaf of hard crusted bread

Chapter Twenty-One

BLANK RECIPE CARDS

Cooking is filled with creation and discovery. If you discover a new recipe on your culinary journey, please use the following recipe cards to keep it handy. Enjoy!

RECIPE NAME ____________________

Serves ____________

Prep Time ____________

Cook Time ____________

Ingredients

Preparation Instructions and Serving Suggestions

RECIPE NAME ________________________

Serves ______________

Prep Time ______________

Cook Time ______________

Ingredients

____

____

____

____

____

____

Preparation Instructions and Serving Suggestions

____

____

____

____

____

____

____

RECIPE NAME ______________________________

Serves ______________

Prep Time ____________

Cook Time ___________

Ingredients

____

____

____

____

____

____

Preparation Instructions and Serving Suggestions

____

____

____

____

____

____

____

RECIPE NAME ______________________________

Serves ______________

Prep Time ______________

Cook Time ______________

Ingredients

Preparation Instructions and Serving Suggestions

RECIPE NAME ____________________

Serves ____________

Prep Time ____________

Cook Time ____________

Ingredients

Preparation Instructions and Serving Suggestions

RECIPE NAME ______________________________

Serves ________________

Prep Time ______________

Cook Time ____________

Ingredients

Preparation Instructions and Serving Suggestions

RECIPE NAME ______________________

Serves ______________

Prep Time ______________

Cook Time ______________

Ingredients

____

____

____

____

____

____

Preparation Instructions and Serving Suggestions

____

____

____

____

____

____

____

GLOSSARY

á la king: food prepared in a creamy white sauce containing mushrooms and red and/or green peppers.

á la mode: food served with ice cream.

al dente: the point in the cooking of pasta at which it is still fairly firm to the tooth; that is, very slightly undercooked.

antipasto: assorted appetizers and relishes, such as olives, anchovies, sliced sausage, artichoke hearts.

appetizer: small portion of a food or drink served before or as the first course of a meal.

aspic: jellied meat juice or a liquid held together with gelatin.

au gratin: food served crusted with breadcrumbs or shredded cheese.

au jus: meat served in its own juice.

bake: to cook food in an oven by dry heat.

barbecue: to roast meat slowly over coals on a spit or framework, or in an oven, basting intermittently with a special sauce.

baste: to spoon pan liquid over meats while they are roasting to prevent surface from drying.

beat: to mix vigorously with a brisk motion with spoon, fork, egg beater, or electric mixer.

bechamel: white sauce of butter, flour, milk, and seasonings.

bisque: thick, creamy soup usually made of shellfish, but sometimes made of puréed vegetables.

blanch: to dip briefly into boiling water.

blend: to stir two or more ingredients together until well mixed.

blintz: crepe stuffed with cheese or other filling and sautéed or baked.

boil: to cook food in water or liquid that is mostly water (at 212°) in which bubbles constantly rise to the surface and burst.

borscht: soup containing beets and other vegetables, usually with a meat stock base.

bouillabaisse: highly seasoned fish soup or chowder containing two or more kinds of fish.

bouillon: clear soup made by simmering meat in water.

bouquet garni: mixture of herbs tied in cheesecloth which are cooked in a mixture and removed before serving.

bourguignon: name applied to dishes containing Burgundy and often braised onions and mushrooms.

braise: to cook slowly with liquid or steam in a covered, heavy pot.

bread, to: to coat with breadcrumbs, usually in combination with egg or other binder.

broil: to cook by direct heat, either under the heat of a broiler, over hot coals, or between two hot surfaces.

broth: thin soup, or a liquid in which meat, fish, or vegetables have been boiled.

canapé: thin piece of bread, toast, etc., spread or topped with cheese, caviar, anchovies, or other foods.

capers: buds from a Mediterranean plant, usually packed in brine and used as a condiment in dressings or sauces.

caramelize: to cook white sugar in a skillet over medium heat, stirring constantly, until sugar forms a golden-brown syrup.

casserole: ovenproof baking dish, usually with a cover; also the food cooked inside it.

cassoulet: casserole of white beans which is baked with herbs and meat.

caviar: the roe (eggs) of sturgeon or other fish, usually served as an appetizer.

charlotte: molded dessert usually formed in a glass dish or a pan that is lined with ladyfingers or pieces of cake.

chop: cut of meat usually attached to a rib.

chop, to: to cut into pieces, with a sharp knife or kitchen shears.

chutney: sauce or relish of East Indian origin containing both sweet and sour ingredients, with spices and other seasonings.

clarified butter: butter that has been melted and chilled. The solid is then lifted away from the liquid and discarded. Clarification heightens the smoke point of butter. Clarified butter will stay fresh in the refrigerator for at least two months.

coat: to cover completely, as in "coat with flour."

cocktail: appetizer; either a beverage or a light, highly seasoned food, served before a meal.

compote: mixed fruit or vegetables, raw or cooked, usually served in "compote" dishes.

condiments: seasonings that enhance the flavor of foods with which they are served.

consomme: clear broth made from meat.

cool: to let food stand at room temperature until not warm to the touch.

coquille: shell or small dish made in the shape of a shell. Used for baking and serving various fish or seafood dishes prepared with a sauce.

court bouillon: highly seasoned broth made with water, vegetables, and seasonings.

cream, to: to blend together, as sugar and butter, until mixture takes on a smooth, cream-like texture.

cream, whipped: cream that has been whipped until it is stiff.

creme de cacao: chocolate-flavored liqueur.

creme de cafe: coffee-flavored liqueur.

creole: dish made with tomatoes and peppers; usually served over rice.

crepes: very thin pancakes.

croquette: minced food, shaped like a ball, patty, cone, or log, bound with a heavy sauce, breaded, and fried.

croutons: cubes of bread, toasted or fried, served with soups or salads.

cube, to: to cut into cube-shaped pieces.

curaçao: orange-flavored liqueur.

cut in, to: to incorporate by cutting or chopping motions, as in cutting shortening into flour for pastry.

demitasse: small cup of coffee served after dinner.

devil, to: to prepare with hot seasoning or sauce.

dice: to cut into small cubes.

dissolve: to mix a dry substance with liquid until the dry substance becomes a part of the solution.

dot: to scatter small bits of butter over top of a food.

dredge: to coat with something, usually flour or sugar.

drippings: fats and juices that come from meat as it cooks.

en papillote: cooked and served in a wrapping of foil or oiled paper. Usually meat or fish is cooked this way.

filé: powder made of sassafras leaves used to season and thicken foods.

filet: boneless piece of meat or fish.

fines herbs: French blend of tarragon, chervil, parsley, and chives.

flambé: to flame, as in crepes suzette or in some meat cookery, using alcohol as the burning agent; flame causes caramelization, enhancing flavor.

flan: in France, a filled pastry; in Spain, a custard.

florentine: food containing or placed upon spinach.

flour, to: to coat with flour.

fold: to add a whipped ingredient, such as cream or egg whites, to another ingredient by a gentle over-and-under movement.

frappé: drink whipped with ice to make a thick, frosty consistency.

fricassee: stew, usually of poultry or veal.

fritter: vegetable or fruit dipped into, or combined with, batter and fried.

garnish: decoration for a food or drink.

giblets: heart, liver, gizzard, and neck of a fowl, often cooked separately.

glaze: (to make a shiny surface) in meat preparation, a gelled broth applied to meat surface; in breads and pastries, a wash of egg or syrup; for doughnuts and cakes, a sugar preparation for coating.

grate: to obtain small particles of food by rubbing on a grater or shredder.

grill: to broil under or over a source of direct heat.

grits: coarsely ground dried corn, served boiled, or boiled and then fried.

gumbo: soup or stew made with okra.

herb: aromatic plant used for seasoning and garnishing foods.

hollandaise: sauce made of butter, egg, and lemon juice or vinegar.

hominy: whole corn grains from which hull and germ are removed.

hors d'oeuvre: appetizer (either a relish or a more elaborate preparation) served before or as the first course of a meal. Usually a finger food.

papillote: wrapping of foil or oiled paper in which a food, usually a meat or fish, is cooked.

parboil: to partially cook in boiling water before final cooking.

pasta: large family of flour-paste products, such as spaghetti, macaroni, and noodles.

pâté: paste made of liver or meat.

petit four: small cake, which has been frosted and decorated.

pilau or pilaf: dish of the Middle East consisting of rice and meat or vegetables cooked in a seasoned stock.

poach: to cook in liquid held below the boiling point.

pot liquor: the liquid in which vegetables have been boiled.

preheat: to turn on oven so that desired temperature will be reached before food is inserted for baking.

prosciutto: ham that has been cured by drying; always sliced paper-thin for serving.

purée: thick sauce or paste made by forcing cooked food through a sieve.

reduce: to boil down, evaporating liquid from a cooked dish.

remoulade: rich mayonnaise-based sauce containing anchovy paste, capers, herbs, and mustard.

render: to melt fat away from surrounding meat.

rind: outer shell or peel of melon or fruit.

roast, to: to cook in oven by dry heat (usually applied to meats or vegetables).

roux: a mixture of butter and flour used to thicken gravies and sauces; it may be white or brown, if mixture is browned before liquid is added.

sauté: to fry food lightly over fairly high heat in a small amount of fat in a shallow, open pan.

scald: (1) to heat milk just below the boiling point; (2) to dip certain foods into boiling water before freezing them (also called blanching).

scallop: bivalve mollusk of which only the muscle hinge is eaten; also to bake a food in a sauce topped with crumbs.

score: to cut shallow gashes on surface of food, as in scoring fat on ham before glazing.

sear: to brown surface of meat over high heat to seal in juices.

set: term used to describe the consistency of gelatin when it has gelled enough to unmold.

shred: break into thread-like or stringy pieces, usually by rubbing over the surface of a vegetable shredder.

simmer: to cook gently at a temperature below boiling point.

skewer: to fasten with wooden or metal pins or skewers.

soak: to immerse in water for a period of time.

soufflé: spongy hot dish, made from a sweet or savory mixture (often milk or cheese), lightened by stiffly beaten egg whites.

steam: to cook food with steam either in a pressure cooker, on a platform in a covered pan, or in a special steamer.

steep: to let food stand in not quite boiling water until the flavor is extracted.

stew: mixture of meat or fish and vegetables cooked by simmering in its own juices and liquid, such as water and/or wine.

stroganoff: meat browned with onion and cooked in sauce of sour cream, seasonings, and usually mushrooms.

syrupy: thickened to about the consistency of egg white.

toast, to: to brown by direct heat, as in a toaster or under broiler.

torte: round cake, sometimes made with breadcrumbs instead of flour.

tortilla: Mexican flat bread made of corn or wheat flour.

toss: to mix together with light tossing motions, in order not to bruise delicate food, such as salad greens.

triple sec: orange-flavored liqueur.

veal: flesh of a milk-fed calf up to 14 weeks of age.

velouté: white sauce made of flour, butter, and a chicken or veal stock, instead of milk.

vinaigrette: cold sauce of oil and vinegar flavored with parsley, finely chopped onions, and other seasonings; served with cold meats or vegetables, and on salads.

whip: to beat rapidly to increase air and increase volume.

RECIPE INDEX

Listed by Main Ingredient in Recipe Title

Cheese (As Appears in Title of Recipe)

Chicken and Fowl

Desserts (Treats and Sweets)

Eggs

Fish and Seafood

Pork

Potatoes

Rice Dishes

Salads, Salsas, and Salad Dressings

Sauces and Gravies

GARDENING INDEX

Gardening Information

Extra Herb Lore, Bits, and Trivia

Herbs—How to Cook with It after You've Grown It

ABOUT THE AUTHORS

Tim Haas and Jan Beane have been cooking with herbs for years and sharing their knowledge at herbal conferences, workshops, and conventions. Together, they host *From The Garden To The Kitchen with Tim and Jan*, a television show combining culinary and gardening endeavors. They also author a syndicated column. Both authors live in Charlotte, North Carolina.